# ENGLISH from the ROOTS UP

Help for Reading, Writing, Spelling, and S.A.T. Scores

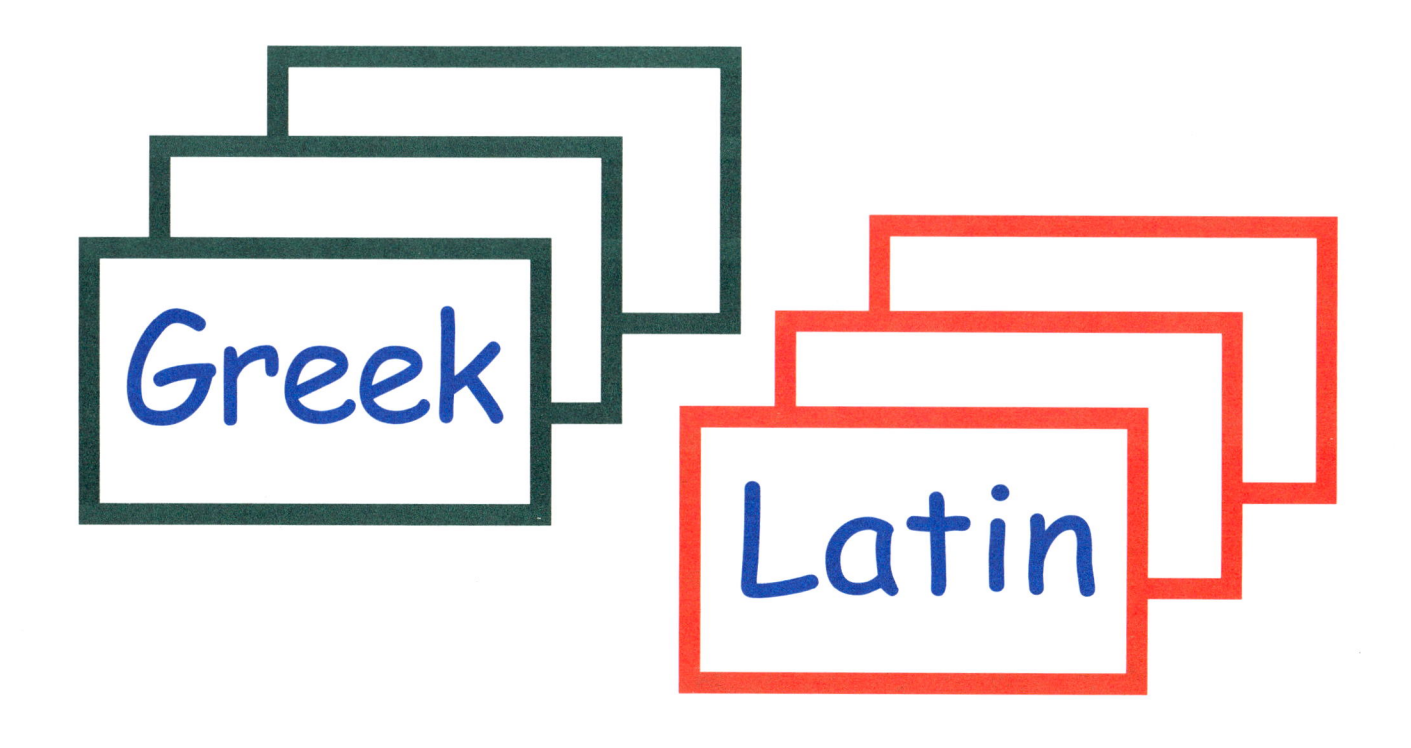

Greek

Latin

Volume II

by Joégil K. Lundquist and Jeanne L. Lundquist

A Publication of LITERACY UNLIMITED
Medina, Washington

Copyright © 2003
by Joégil K. Lundquist and Jeanne L. Lundquist

All rights reserved. No part of this book may be reproduced or transmitted in any form or by any means, electronic or mechanical, including photocopying or any information storage and retrieval system, without permission in writing from the Publisher.

Literacy Unlimited Publications
P.O. Box 278
Medina, Washington, 98039-0278

ISBN: 1-885942-31-1

First Printing November 2003
Second Printing September 2005

Printed in the United States of America

# TABLE OF CONTENTS

Dedications ........................................................................ i

Acknowledgments ............................................................ ii

What's in Volume II? ....................................................... iii

The Roots Rap ................................................................. iv

Preface .............................................................................. v

How to Use This Book .................................................... ix

Volume II Numerical Index ........................................... xiii

Volume II Alphabetical Index ....................................... xiv

Pronouncing Latin Words .............................................. xv

Pronunciation Guide by Nora MacDonald .................. xvi

Parts of Speech by Nora MacDonald ......................... xviii

Roman Numerals ........................................................... xix

The Greek Alphabet ....................................................... xx

Greek and Latin Root words ..................................... 1-100

Appendix I - Cats or Dogs First? You Decide ............. 101

Appendix II - Quick Alphabetical Index to Volume I ..... 105

Bibliography ................................................................. 106

# DEDICATIONS

## *To Elsa MacPhee (Midge) Bowman*

Who, while serving as Director of the Elementary Division of The Bush School, supported and encouraged the development of our program of Classical Studies in second grade - for her far-seeing, Janus-like understanding that students can face what lies ahead with better judgment and perspicacity when they have learned to cast discerning eyes on what has gone before.

JKL

## *To Lynn Ennis Iozzo*

Who, as my Middle School Latin teacher at Bush School, cracked open so many mysteries of English vocabulary and grammar for me. Studying derivatives in Lynn's class made Latin relevant to everyday life, as I heard the words we studied in class repeated on the radio, in newspapers, textbooks, and everywhere around me. I found myself constantly drawing on concepts I'd learned in Lynn's class in subsequent English classes, as well as Spanish and Italian classes. Without Lynn's gentle introduction to the five declensions in Latin, I would probably have run screaming from the room when I encountered *seven* declensions in the Czech language. Her contagious enthusiasm for Latin, and for the modern descendants of the Romans, kindled in me a desire to travel to Italy, a desire which has continued to flare and intensify since my first visit there during college.

JLL

# ACKNOWLEDGMENTS

We have many people to whom we owe a debt of gratitude for help in completing this **second volume** of *ENGLISH FROM THE ROOTS UP*. Our editors, **Mary Anagnost** and **Nora MacDonald** pulled us back from the brink and prevented us from committing the errors in Latin and Greek we were, now and then, tempted to commit. **Nancy Larsen** and **Dan Watkins** pounded home lessons in punctuation and clarity which will make using this book far easier for everyone. **Scott Davis**, as he has over many years past, helped in hundreds of ways, and wielded a verbal whip, urging us, among other things, to "get on with it!" **Jeannine Rogel**, who in years past had taught the root words in Volume I, did us the honor of trying out some of these new words in her fifth grade classroom as they spewed forth from our printer. The enthusiasm of her students was a great encouragement to us and we agreed to begin this volume with the root word of their choice – *Canis* – dog. (You will see the debating points they used to arrive at this decision in Appendix I.) We are grateful to **Jeanne Bluechel** too, whose grandson, Patrick, was a student in Jeannine's class, who introduced us to Jeannine and all her wonderful students.

To **Captain Robert Hempstead** and **Tish Davis**, we owe our gratitude for their expertise in piloting us through the fascinating language of the sea and the use of the sextant in navigation.

To **Rev. Michael Hodges** who, from 3000 miles away, keeps our web site running smoothly and his wife, **Koky Hodges** who gives needed encouragement and great ideas.

We are grateful to **Jeanne Blue**, and to **Letitia and Don Davis**, for keeping Literacy Unlimited going so we could have time to research and write; to **Carolyn Lacy**, **Mike Sorenson, Norio and Miyoko Yamazaki**, for shepherding the manuscript into printable form and then printing it "in time."

Finally, heartfelt thanks to my husband (and Jeannie's dad), **Lou Lundquist**, for making everything possible. Much gratitude to our son (and Jeannie's brother), **Deke Lundquist** and his beloved wife, **Annie**, who have supportively lived next door throughout these writing years; and to their children, **Lucie**, five, and **Tellier**, three, who have played on the swings outside our office window and constantly reminded us why we wanted to write this book in the first place. (Cat lovers that they are, they would probably have chosen *feles* – cat as the first word in the book, but as we reminded them, dogs need and demand attention whereas cats could hardly care less! After all as someone online pointed out, "Dogs have owners; cats have staff.") And lastly, our gratitude goes to **Buff** and **Charlie**, our comfort-seeking Balinese cats, who took responsibility for keeping us on task by sitting on the lap of whoever was typing at the computer and protesting all interruptions.

Thank you ALL!

Joégil and Jeannie Lundquist,
Medina, Washington,
November 2003


Joégil K. Lundquist

# WHAT'S IN VOLUME II?

One hundred new root words – 67 Latin and 33 Greek – with English derivatives for you to teach to your students. They are a little more advanced than the collection that appeared in Volume I – but we believe they are still easy for students from 4th grade up to understand and enjoy.

Just for fun, and because we've had so many requests for it, we have included THE ROOTS RAP, which students of all ages have enjoyed. We hope you enjoy it too.

There is a section on HOW TO USE THIS BOOK with suggestions on how to present the lessons to your class. But they are just that – suggestions. However you, the teacher, decide to teach your children – the personal imprint you will always impart to the lessons, your enthusiasm, and your sense of enjoyment will in the end affect the value your students will take away with them – and the extent to which they will continue to profit from these lessons in Latin and Greek vocabulary throughout the rest of their years in school – and beyond. If you, by chance, hear that they are telling other students or their parents about the words they are learning – you may consider your lessons wildly successful.

There is a NUMERICAL INDEX of all the words just as they appear from 1 to 100. There are also separate ALPHABETICAL INDICES of the Latin and Greek root words to make it easy to find the one you are looking for.

There is a PRONUNCIATION GUIDE prepared by our Latin teacher collaborator, Nora MacDonald. We have scattered her phonetic pronunciation spellings to the appropriate pages throughout the book – on the top line of the derivative boxes – right next to the definition of the root word. This way you don't have to keep turning the pages of the book back and forth to find the pronunciation while you are trying to put the lessons on the board and help students. Nora has also provided us with a useful reference page on the PARTS OF SPEECH from which you may want to prepare a lesson for your students.

The page on ROMAN NUMERALS from Volume I is included, as is the page on the GREEK ALPHABET since you will need these reference pages handy as you are teaching the root word lessons.

As we were researching these root word pages, we "beta tested" them by delivering the animal pages to a class of fifth graders at nearby Medina School taught by classics enthusiast, Jeannine Rogel. We gave her boys and girls their choice of which word should begin the book – CANIS - dog or FELES - cat. They took the challenge seriously and wrote persuasive essays to back up their choices and then held a debate to try to convince each other to vote for their favorite animal. A vote was taken and the rest is history. We enjoyed their "selling points" and present them as APPENDIX I right after word #100 DOKEIN.

APPENDIX II gives you a NUMERICAL INDEX of all the root words from VOLUME I. If you don't have a copy of Volume I, you may want to refer to it from time to time.

Finally, the bibliography lists the books we consulted to prepare these root word and derivative lessons. You may want to browse through them as you embark on your own excursions into the Classical world. Bon Voyage!

# THE ROOTS RAP

*[Have fun with this! Snap fingers, clap hands, tap feet, drum on table, whatever...]*

LATIN is a language that's had a bum rap!
It delivers lots of benefits right into your lap!
It isn't stone dead like some folks say -
In fact we all are usin' it every single day!
But never underestimate the power of a rhyme!
It killed a healthy subject in the middle of its prime!
Some lazy nerd put together four lines
When he hadn't done his homework in the school salt mines.

He said, "Latin is a language - as dead as it can be!
It killed off all the Romans - and now it's killin' me!"
Well, his friends began to laugh, yes, they commenced to snicker -
And the ridicule of Latin was deadlier than likker!
Then the French and the Spanish looked at Latin askance.
They said, "Kids! Drop Latin! WE got the ROMANCE!
You can talk to your friends, you can travel far and wide!"
So - the kids dropped Latin (they were taken for a ride)!

They got along in Canada and down in Mexico
But at home, the English language they didn't really know!
They learned a few words - couple syllables was tops.
If it had four letters, they could use it in the shops!
They hung out in the malls and they dyed their hair -
And they played punk rock to the parents' dispair!
THEN one little kid yelled "I GOT A ROOT!
It'll grow me a VOCABULARY! What a HOOT!

"Those Romans and Greeks, they were so COOL!
They made up the words we got down at the school!
They had 'PHOTO' and 'GRAPH' - you know what they mean?
They mean *light,- draw and write* and the Greek cards are green!
You put 'em together and they make PHOTOGRAPH
'Light drawing a picture' - now that's a laugh!
Then you haul in 'TELE', which means 'far from home'
And you get TELEPHOTO, TELEGRAPH, TELEPHONE!

We put our Latin words on the red-bordered cards -
They had 'AUDIO' and 'VIDEO' - they're not so hard!
And 'PATER. MATER. FRATER' - the whole family!
And the kids in the class are 'DISCIPULI'!"
Now you make your own collection and learn 'em real well
And how far you'll go, nobody can tell!
But the old Greeks and Romans from the ancient days
Left YOU a RICH HERITAGE - to keep ALWAYS!

© 1996 Joégil K. Lundquist.
All rights reserved -May be reproduced only with publisher's written permission .

# PREFACE

One of my favorite books as a child was a story called ***Paddle to the Sea*** by Holling C. Holling. For those who have never encountered this gem, it's the story of a native Indian boy, who carves and paints a model of an Indian paddling a little canoe. The boy sets his Paddle Person in the snow before the thaw in the Nipigon region of Canada, above Lake Superior, starting him on a journey which the boy hopes will carry the little canoe to the Atlantic Ocean.

To discourage people from interfering with the voyage, the boy carves a sign on the hull of his model, "Please put me back in water. I am Paddle to the Sea." Paddle meets with all sorts of adventures (beavers, a sawmill, waterfalls, etc.) along the way as he meanders through the Great Lakes and down the St. Lawrence River, and the trip provides an informal and entertaining geography lesson.

Several months into his mission, Paddle has lost most of his original paint and gets a new paint job and a coat of varnish from a helpful soul in the Coast Guard. The Coast Guard man also affixes a plaque to the bottom of Paddle's canoe, on which others who fish him out of the water along his journey can engrave the name of their city, so that Paddle's journey can be traced by those who find him later. After four years and several thousand indirect miles, Paddle finally reaches his destination, the great wide Atlantic Ocean.

Like ***Paddle to the Sea,*** each of the Greek and Latin roots in this book, and those in ***Volume I,*** have traveled an epic journey of thousands of years and several thousand miles to arrive in the ocean of our modern English language. (Just as the Atlantic touches many countries, so these roots have found their way into many languages.) Some roots seem to have been battered almost beyond recognition by the waves and rocks along their journey, while others seem to have arrived still sporting their original coat of paint.

A good unabridged dictionary provides a record of each derivative's (***de***-down from + ***rivus*** – brook, stream) voyage down river from its root, to show the ports of call it visited on its journey into English (such as a stopover in Old French). The Oxford English Dictionary even attempts to pinpoint the year a word was first used with a particular meaning and who used it that way.

The more we know about each word's journey into English, the more our own language comes alive and the more we care about, and the more fun we have, using the right words well.

When I entered the sixth grade, I was given a choice of which "foreign" language to study: Latin, Spanish, or French. I put "foreign" in quotes, because I now understand that Latin is so integral to the study of English that it really ought to be part of any English curriculum. Fortunately, I had parents who recognized this fact, so I was *strongly encouraged* to take Latin. My parents said I would be free to study any language that I wanted, *after* I had taken three years of Latin. After studying Latin, I was very grateful to them for their insistence.

Have you ever had the experience of learning a new word that you don't remember hearing before, then all of a sudden, once you know what it means, you start hearing and seeing it everywhere? My Latin class gave me these little "Aha!" experiences often, as I

began to recognize derivatives of my vocabulary words from Latin class in everyday conversations and everywhere in all kinds of media. I began to wonder how many times I actually had heard a word in conversations before, but because I had no mental hook to hang it on, it didn't register and I didn't remember it. I also wondered what I had been missing by allowing the words I didn't understand to wash over me.

With each year of Latin, I began to understand more of the adult conversations around me, and felt that people weren't talking over my head as much any more. My vocabulary workbook for English class seemed more like a review of words I already knew from Latin class. When I finally had the freedom to study Spanish in High School, studying Spanish vocabulary was like bumping into old friends in new back-to-school clothes. I also saw other students and friends who hadn't had the opportunity to take Latin struggle with strange new vocabulary.

Whenever my college roommate asked me how to spell a word or what a word meant, I often found myself supplying the root from which the word came, if I knew it. (I suppose I had unconsciously picked up my Mom's practice of doing this for me.) Understanding that my motivation wasn't to spout what I knew, but to help make her studies easier, my roommate began prompting me to tell her which root a word came from, and would tease me by acting disappointed if I couldn't furnish it.

During my senior year in college, ten years of daydreams about traveling to Italy finally became reality with an opportunity to study for a quarter in Rome. As I stood at the ancient floor level inside the Coliseum in Rome, in awe of the technology and scale of building the Romans were capable of two millennia ago; I felt a hair-tingling feeling of belonging, in spite of having no known Italian ancestry. I felt connected to the Romans by virtue of having inherited significant elements of their language, their legal system, and their culture.

My fascination with the Romans and my appreciation for having studied Latin deepened when living and working in Central Europe. As a teacher of English as a foreign language to students at Charles University in what was, at the time, Prague, Czechoslovakia, I was grateful whenever I ran across any word which was even remotely familiar within the Czech language. When I recognized the word "filozoficka" (philosophical) on one of the University buildings, I felt the long arm of the Roman Empire tapping me on the shoulder to remind me that even this seemingly remote region of their former empire bore the remnants of Rome's influence, and had in fact eventually become the seat of the Holy Roman Empire.

My students, candidates for degrees in natural sciences, were required to take two years of language before passing a written and oral proficiency exam. Some of my students were obviously out to get by with the minimum amount of effort needed to pass the requirement, while others were highly motivated and had progressed beyond the level of the University's selected textbook. In an effort to provide a challenge for my more advanced students, I asked my Mom to send me a copy of her book, ***English from the Roots Up, Volume I***, and began to introduce the Greek and Latin roots to my second-year students. I was thrilled when they took to the roots with enthusiasm and shared with me that the information was helpful in their other classes, since so many of the scientific names they studied were in Latin. Their response encouraged me to test the roots with my first-year students. I found that even the "minimal effort" students sat up with interest and began to take notes and ask good questions when I introduced the roots. I was excited to be able to

provide them with tools which they would be able to use on their own after they tested out of the minimum language requirement.

Czech is a beautiful Slavic language, which thankfully has quite regular phonetic pronunciation, such that a foreigner can learn how to pronounce almost any word they read within a short period of study, relative to other languages. That is, with the exception of the letter "ř" ("rzh" - *roll the r - as in the composer, Dvořak*), which notoriously trips people up so badly that the Czechs were able to identify Nazi spies by their difficulty with the sound. Despite the phonetic pronunciation, comprehension and correct construction of a grammatical sentence is an entirely different matter! I was grateful to have been exposed to the five declensions in Latin before wandering into the linguistic fun house of seven declensions (and two different plurals) in Czech. I can't say that I became proficient at speaking Czech, though I did find the Czechs to be remarkably tolerant of and graciously encouraging to any foreigner attempting to communicate in their language.

Many native English speakers, as well as foreigners, have expressed frustration and confusion over the variety of ways different sounds are spelled in English. However, those who, in a fit of pique and exasperation, wish to overhaul the English language just to make it easier to spell (giving each sound only one uniform symbol) would rob our children of the culture and heritage innate in our spelling. Our quirky spelling is full of fascinating clues to the history of words, and how their original and/or metaphoric meaning arrived in our language. For instance, if we dropped the c from **sci**ence, in order to make it easier for some people to spell the word, then we would lose the clue that it comes from the Latin word *scio* – to know (see ***Volume I***, p. 97).

There are some who wish to establish one way of spelling the sound "sh," complaining that "ti," "si," and "ci" are unnecessary and confusing. But, if you change con**sci**ous to "conshus," as some would suggest as an easier-to-spell alternative, you would lose the root *scio*, which is the clue to meaning. Correlatively, if the word nation were overhauled to become "nashun," the loss of the "*t*" means that someone who learned the word "nashun" would not have the immediate clue that the meaning of the word derived from *natus*, the past participle of *nasci* – *to be born*, - (look for this root when ***Volume III*** becomes available!) is related to in***nat***e (something *born* in someone), neo-***nat***al (new*born*), and ***Nat***ivity (*birth*, specifically the *birth* of Christ, when capitalized). Those who know the Latin root *natus* means *to be born*, may even be able to figure out, without much effort, that an Italian who wishes them "*Buon Natale*" is wishing them "Good Nativity" or "Merry Christmas."

Those well-meaning, but short-sighted individuals who suggest a one-symbol-for-one-sound makeover for English spelling would unwittingly make English more difficult to learn, by obscuring the clues to meaning that lie in the ancient roots of our rich linguistic heritage. While their new spelling system might make it easy to *pronounce* the symbols on a written page, the reader would have no clue as to the *meaning* of the words the page contained. As my experience with the Czech language taught me, *being able to pronounce what you see on a page does not mean that you can comprehend what you read!*

Children need to be introduced to a good system of phonics to help them sound out words (such as the Orton phonograms used in Romalda Spalding's ***The Writing Road to Reading,*** or the updated and expanded version by The Riggs Institute in ***The Writing and***

***Spelling Road to Reading and Thinking***). Once they master the phonograms, they should be introduced to Greek and Latin root words which help them form mental images of the meanings of English words. The more roots they know and recognize, the easier it will be for them to figure out what a word is if they've never seen it before. If they are given the tools to feel competent and independent in their study of English words, then they are on their way to being comfortable and voracious lifelong readers and self-educators. With each root that a student learns, a mental storage box is labeled with that root in which multiple derivatives can be stored.

Imagine a room in which several thousand of the most common words in English have been written on separate pieces of paper and thrown on the floor haphazardly. Then imagine one whole wall of this room being shelves full of clear shoebox-sized plastic storage bins. In learning to read, a child is essentially asked to clean up the mess on the floor of this room by learning to recognize and differentiate between all those thousands of words, and to put them away in the right box so that he or she can find them again and read and write them from memory. Without being given the proper tools (such as phonograms to be able to find out what the words are, and roots to figure out what the words mean and how they are related), many children would understandably conclude that the job was just too hard and give up. This is essentially what has happened to cause the huge problem of functional illiteracy facing our country today. So many adults gave up on reading as children when asked to decipher words without having been given the tools to decode them. Give them the code! Giving students access to the roots of their language helps them to organize their mental storage system so they can access words when they need them.

Since Latin has been eased out of most foreign language departments, many students have been cut off from vital information they need to understand the heritage and culture inherent in their language. Those who wanted to get rid of Latin labeled it elitist, and then, by getting rid of it in public schools, ensured that *only* the children of the elite would have access to it in private schools. Those who criticized Latin had likely never studied it, so they couldn't have realized how much they and their children would miss by not having access to it. It's time to level the playing field by giving everyone access to the vibrant pictures that comprise our language. One of the strengths of our language has been its ability to adapt and grow as it absorbs ideas from diverse cultures. When new words are coined for new technologies, companies often use old familiar roots which will help the public get an idea of what their product does.

The desire to enable as many children as possible to understand their language at the earliest age possible was the impetus behind ***Volume I*** of ***English from the Roots Up***. That same desire has fueled the research and writing of ***Volume II***. Joégil and I had a whale of a good time developing this second volume in order to introduce the next hundred root words to you and your students. Hopefully, you'll have as much fun presenting this new material to your students as we've had in researching it!

Jeannie Lundquist
Medina, Washington
© 2003

# HOW TO USE THIS BOOK

If you have already taught the lessons in Volume I to your students, you have undoubtedly devised your own method of how to use the 100 words we have researched and prepared for you here in Volume II. If, however, you have picked up this book without having seen Volume I, and if you want to begin immediately with this book of 100 more advanced root words for your students who have reached the fourth grade or higher, let us make a few suggestions.

Let us encourage you to find or send for a copy of Volume I and introduce the first 100 lessons to your children before going on. The words selected for Volume II are meant to follow on from the lessons already learned in Volume I, and your students will find it easier going if they can build on that solid foundation. Many of the lessons in this book refer to lessons already presented in Volume I. The instructions for presenting the words in classroom sessions in Volume I are for younger children – in grades two or three. Even in the upper grades, however, we encourage you to have your students create the sets of flashcards which they can study and review all through their school days. They will gain considerable value from this effort and many of our own students tell us they still have their collections now that they are in college and a few are using them to teach their own children.

In any case, whether you begin with Volume I or Volume II, you will want to gather some materials and have them ready before your first session with your students.

1 – A pack of 100 or more 3X5 index cards for each student in the class.

2 – Several sets (depending on the number of students in your class) of RED, GREEN and BLUE Watercolor Magic Markers for the Red and Green borders which the students will put on the cards to identify them as "Red for Roman (Latin)" and "Green for Greek"; BLUE for YOU to print the root word on the unlined front of the card.

3 – An index card file box for each student in which to keep the completed cards together. If these cannot be provided by the school or the parents of the students, you can use clean (NOT second hand!) zip-loc plastic sandwich bags or even simply rubber bands, but the file boxes are much to be preferred!

4 – RED, GREEN, and BLUE chalk for putting the definition of the Latin or Greek words and their derivatives on the chalkboard for the children to copy onto the lined side of their own index cards. Or RED, GREEN, and BLUE overhead markers if you prefer to use an overhead projector so that you can face your students as you write.

5 – Several large unabridged dictionaries with good etymology entries showing exactly where each word in the English language originated. Part of the value of these lessons is that the children will become more aware of where words come from and "at home" in answering many of their own questions by a skillful and experienced use of the dictionary. If your budget will allow it, the "Mount Olympus of dictionaries," the 20 volume Oxford English Dictionary will reward you daily for every minute you can spare to browse its pages. Aspire to it! Save for it! Acquire it! (Need we say more?)

6 – A long file box for 3X5 cards (available in stationary stores) for you to keep extra copies of each root word card you have introduced. You are then ready to provide an up-to-date set of cards to any child who joins your class in the weeks or months after the school year has begun. Assign to the new student a willing and competent student helper whose collection is complete and who is able to explain and assist in copying the definitions and derivations onto the backs of the newcomer's cards. Don't do this copying FOR the new student. He or she will gain much more benefit and remember much more by writing the definitions and derivations for himself or herself.

STUDENTS PUT THE RED AND GREEN BORDERS ON THE CARDS.
Encourage children to volunteer to use spare moments putting the red and green borders neatly on the white index cards so they will look like the words pictured on each of the 100 root word pages in the book. (This is a very satisfying pastime.) Our classroom always had a small devoted group of card makers who quietly improved moments between classes or made the most of rainy day recesses making red and green bordered cards awaiting a root word.

YOU PRINT THE LATIN OR GREEK WORDS ON THE CARDS IN BLUE OR BLACK.
We found that the children like them better when the Latin or Greek words are printed on the front of the cards by you. That way, they all look alike, and children tend to take better care of them when you have expended this effort on their behalf. Make enough of each word for the class and a few extra to keep in reserve in your long file box for newcomers to the class.

BEGIN THE LESSON BY PUTTING THE ROOT WORD ON THE BOARD.
Begin the teaching session by putting the word for the day on the board and outlining it with red or green chalk, identifying it as Latin or Greek. The pages in this book show what the front and back of the index cards should look like. We tried to keep the definitions for the derivations short so they would fit on the cards. You may have to limit the number of derivative words you can present, depending on the age of your children and their ability to print small letters.

USE MANUSCRIPT PRINT, RATHER THAN CURSIVE WRITING, ON THE BACKS OF THE CARDS.
The cards are neater and more legible in the long run (and look more like the print in a book) if they are done in manuscript printing rather than in cursive writing – at any grade level. We found that many students soon began their own classes among their friends and younger siblings and were using their collection of cards from which to teach – so having them correctly done is important.

EXPLAIN DEFINITIONS AND DERIVIATIONS
The English words DEFINITION and DERIVATION sound similar to children. It's a good idea to explain the Latin roots of these words to them before you begin the first lesson so they will be able to discern their very different meanings. Then you and the children can use these words with confidence.

DEFINITIONS
<u>Definition</u> comes from the Latin words <u>de</u> – down from, away from + <u>finis</u> – boundary, border, limit. So a definition limits or puts a border (or fence!) around the meaning of a word, separating it from what it does not mean.

DERIVATIONS
Derivation comes from the Latin words de – down from, away from, + rivus – brook, stream, river. So, literally, a derivation would be a drawing off of water from a main stream (as in irrigation). When we speak of words as "derivations" we are drawing off some of that ancient mainstream (or ROOT) meaning and putting it to use is our modern English language.

Perhaps someone could get some information from the library about irrigation and how people have used it through history and report to the class about it. Students can keep notebooks for their notes on such reports as these done by their classmates on concrete concepts which underlie so many of our modern terms. They will learn to VISUALIZE in this way – the prime component of reading comprehension. "Oh yes! I see!"

EXPLAIN METAPHOR
In DEFINITION and DERIVATION you have two beautiful and clear examples of a METAPHOR. A METAPHOR describes a new process or an abstract idea in terms of something known and concrete in order to visualize or image the new process or idea in thought. Piaget estimates that children become capable of abstract thinking at about the age of twelve. However, a deep understanding of the METAPHORS we use in our language brings children along toward that mature level of abstract thinking earlier by allowing them to manipulate abstract ideas with the help of concrete concepts – like the ones in the words definition (a border or fence around meaning) and derivation (a brook or rivulet drawn off from the main stream or root meaning). Do take the time to draw pictures on the board to illustrate these derivative words in concrete terms so that you develop the children's thinking skills along with their vocabularies. (Use pictures, models, visual media aids, field trips, whatever it takes, to make the concept vivid and memorable. The whole advertising world does it – why shouldn't we?)

THE DEFINITION OF THE ROOT WORD GOES ON THE TOP (RED) LINE.
Put the ENGLISH MEANING (the definition of the Latin or Greek root word) on the board and underline it in RED. This helps children remember to put the meaning on the top line (which is red) on the back of their index cards.

THE DERIVATIONS GO ON THE BLUE LINES.
The derivations go on the blue lines. Each new derivative word should start a new line at the left edge of the card like the models on each page of this book. If they are written haphazardly, they will be hard to study later on, and the collection will not become the source of pride and aid to accomplishment which it can be.

THE ORDER OF PRESENTATION OF ROOT WORDS IS UP TO YOU.
The following pages have been assembled so as to make it easy for you to teach root word lessons without having to study and prepare ahead of time. There is nothing sacred about the order in which you present them. Feel free to pick and choose those that appeal to you most, or whatever dovetails well with other subjects studied or current events in the news.

We have organized the words this way:

Words 1-10 are animal words. Children are always interested in these so they should get you off to a good start.

Words 11-57 are mostly pairs of words which can be related in some way to each other such as AMPHI and AMBI, the Greek and Latin words for both; CIRCUM and KYKLOS, the Latin and Greek words for around and circle; IATROS and MEDICUS, the Greek and Latin words for physician or doctor. When these pairs can be compared and contrasted, they are easier to remember and will help later in identifying unknown English vocabulary words.

Words 58-60, NOVUS, ORDO, and SAECULUM, are placed together because they illuminate the meaning of the Latin phrase found on a dollar bill - which is a mystery to most of the people who handle our currency from day to day. We thought it was fun to shed some light on it so the children can initiate discussions with their friends and families.

Words 61-70 present the ordinal numbers from first to tenth. The cardinal numbers are found in Volume I. Just as very small children enjoy learning to count from one to ten, these sets of ten Latin numbers (both cardinal and ordinal) are natural collections for ease of memorizing and long term recollection.

Words 71-100 are a somewhat random collection with a few Latin and Greek pairs such as VOX and LOQUI relating to speaking; SOLUS and MONOS meaning alone; LABORO and ERGON, having to do with work. The rest are simply words which we thought would be accessible and enjoyable for children in the upper elementary grades – as well as, of course, students of any age or grade, in middle school, high school, or college.

We hope you will have as much fun presenting these root words to your students as Jeannie and I have had researching and writing these pages and that they will enhance the skill and enjoyment of your children's reading and scholarship for the rest of their lives.

Joégil Lundquist
Medina, Washington
© November 2003

# NUMERICAL INDEX – VOLUME II

1 – **CANIS** – L. – dog
2 – **FELES** – L. – cat
3 – **LEON** – G. – lion
4 – **EQUUS** – L. – horse
5 – **CABALLUS** – L. – horse
6 – **HIPPOS** – G. – horse
7 – **PORCUS** – L. – pig
8 – **ORNIS** – G. – bird
9 – **AVIS** – L. – bird
10 – **GREX, GREGIS** – L. – herd, group
11 – **OMNIS** – L. – all
12 – **AMPHI** – G. – both
13 – **AMBI** – L. – both
14 – **EU** – G. – well, good
15 – **MALUS** – L. – bad, ugly, evil, ill
16 – **E, EX** – L. – out of, from
17 – **ARCHOS** – G. – leader, chief, beginning
18 – **ARCUS** – L. – bow, arc
19 – **CIRCUM** – L. – around, about
20 – **KYKLOS** – G. – ring, circle, wheel
21 – **PERI** – G. – around
22 – **THEOS** – G. – god
23 – **DEUS** – L. – god
24 – **DIVINUS** – L. – god-like
25 – **HOMO, HOMINIS** – L. – man, human
26 – **ANTHROPOS** – G. – man, mankind
27 – **VIR** – L. – man
28 – **FEMINA** – L. – woman
29 – **INFANS, INFANTIS** – L. – speechless
30 – **PAIS, PAIDOS** – G. – child
31 – **SCHOLE** – G. – leisure, free time
32 – **LUDO, LUSUS** – L. – play, mock
33 – **IATROS** – G. – physician, comforter
34 – **MEDICUS** – L. – doctor
35 – **SANUS** – L. – healthy, free of disease
36 – **HOLOS** – G. – whole, entire, complete
37 – **RHINOS** – G. – nose, snout
38 – **CORNU** – L. – horn
39 – **DERMA** – G. – skin, hide, shell
40 – **CUTIS** – L. – skin, hide
41 – **COR, CORDIS** – L. – heart
42 – **DORSUM** – L. – back
43 – **ATHLON** – G. – prize, award
44 – **AGON** – G. – contest, struggle
45 – **DROMOS** – G. – running, race course
46 – **MONS, MONTIS** – L. – mountain
47 – **HUMUS** – L. – earth, soil
48 – **FOLIUM** – L. – leaf
49 – **SAL, SALIS** – L. – salt
50 – **MARE** – L. – sea, ocean

51 – **NAUS** – G. – ship, boat
52 – **NAVIS** – L. – ship, boat
53 – **HOMOS** – G. – same
54 – **HETEROS** – G. – other, different
55 – **CARDO, CARDINIS** – L. – hinge
56 – **PORTA** – L. – door, gate, entry
57 – **PORTO, PORTATUM** – L. – carry
58 – **NOVUS** – L. – new
59 – **ORDO, ORDINIS** – L. – row, order
60 – **SAECULUM** – L. – age, century
61 – **PRIMUS** – L. – first
62 – **SECUNDUS** – L. – second
63 – **TERTIUS** – L. – third
64 – **QUARTUS** – L. – fourth
65 – **QUINTUS** – L. – fifth
66 – **SEXTUS** – L. – sixth
67 – **SEPTIMUS** – L. – seventh
68 – **OCTAVUS** – L. – eighth
69 – **NONUS** – L. – ninth
70 – **DECIMUS** – L. – tenth
71 – **ELECTRON** – G. – amber
72 – **GRADUS** – L. – step, degree
73 – **PLUS, PLURIS** – L. – more, many
74 – **AKROS** – G. – top-most, extreme
75 – **KATA** – G. – down, against, completely
76 – **ANA** – G. – up, back, again
77 – **DUCO, DUCTUM** – L. – draw, attract, lead
78 – **AGO, ACTUM** – L. – do, act, perform
79 – **PENDO, PENSUM** – L. – hang, weigh
80 – **HYPER** – G. – above, overly, beyond
81 – **HYPO** – G. – under, below
82 – **SUPER** – L. – above, over
83 – **SUB** – L. – under
84 – **RUMPO, RUPTUM** – L. – break
85 – **PAX, PACIS** – L. – peace
86 – **SPECTO, SPECTATUM** – L. – look at, see
87 – **VOX, VOCIS** – L – voice
88 – **LOQUI** – L. – speak
89 – **FELIX, FELICIS** – L. – happy
90 – **FIDES** – L. – faith
91 – **SOLUS** – L. – alone
92 – **MONOS** – G. – alone, solitary
93 – **RIDEO, RISUM** – L. – laugh, make fun of
94 – **LABORO, LABORATUM** – L. – work
95 – **ERGON** – G. – work
96 – **DURUS** – L. – hard
97 – **BELLUM** – L. – war, combat, fight
98 – **BARBAROS** – G. – foreign
99 – **ORTHOS** – G. – straight, correct
100 – **DOKEIN** – G. – think, have an opinion

© 2003 J&J Lundquist

# ALPHABETICAL INDEX - VOLUME II
(Page numbers in parentheses)

## LATIN ROOT WORDS

**AGO, ACTUM** – L. – do, act, perform (78)
**AMBI** – L. – both (13)
**ARCUS** – L. – bow, arc (18)
**AVIS** – L. – bird (9)
**BELLUM** – L. – war, fight (97)
**CABALLUS** – L. – horse (5)
**CANIS** – L. – dog (1)
**CARDO, CARDINIS** – L. – hinge (55)
**CIRCUM** – L. – around, about (19)
**COR, CORDIS** – L. – heart (41)
**CORNU** – L. – horn (38)
**CUTIS** – L. – skin, hide (40)
**DECIMUS** – L. – tenth (70)
**DEUS** – L. – god (23)
**DIVINUS** – L. – god-like (24)
**DORSUM** – L. – back (42)
**DUCO, DUCTUM** – L. – lead, attract (77)
**DURUS** – L. – hard (96)
**EQUUS** – L. – horse (4)
**E, EX** – L. – out of, from (16)
**FELES** – L. – cat (2)
**FELIX, FELICIS** – L. – happy (89)
**FEMINA** – L. – woman (28)
**FIDES** – L. – faith (90)
**FOLIUM** – L. – leaf (48)
**GRADUS** – L. – step, degree (72)
**GREX, GREGIS** – L. – herd (10)
**HOMO, HOMINIS** – L. – man (25)
**HUMUS** – L. – earth, soil (47)
**INFANS, INFANTIS** – L. – speechless (29)
**LABORO, LABORATUM** – L. – work (94)
**LOQUOR, LOCUTUM** – L. – speak (88)
**LUDO, LUSUS** – L. – play, mock (32)
**MALUS** – L. – bad, ugly, ill (15)
**MARE** – L. – sea, ocean (50)
**MEDICUS** – L. – doctor (34)
**MONS, MONTIS** – L. – mountain (46)
**NAVIS** – L. – ship, boat (52)
**NONUS** – L. – ninth (69)
**NOVUS** – L. – new (58)
**OCTAVUS** – L. – eighth (68)
**OMNIS** – L. – all (11)
**ORDO, ORDINIS** – L. row, order (59)
**PAX, PACIS** – L. – peace (85)
**PENDO, PENSUM** – L. – hang, weigh (79)
**PLUS, PLURIS** – L. – more, many (73)
**PORCUS** – L. – pig (7)
**PORTA** – L. – door, gate, entry (56)
**PORTO, PORTATUM** – L. – carry (57)
**PRIMUS** – L. – first (61)
**QUARTUS** – L. – fourth (64)
**QUINTUS** – L. – fifth (65)
**RIDEO, RISUM** – L. – laugh at (93)
**RUMPO, RUPTUM** – L. – break (84)
**SAL, SALIS** – L. – salt (49)
**SAECULUM** – L. – age, century (60)
**SANUS** – L. – health (35)
**SECUNDUS** – L. – second (62)
**SEPTIMUS** – L. – seventh (67)
**SEXTUS** – L. – sixth (66)
**SOLUS** – L. – alone (91)
**SPECTO, SPECTATUM** – L. – look at (86)
**SUB** – L. – under (83)
**SUPER** – L. – above, over (82)
**TERTIUS** – L. – third (63)
**VIR** – L. – man (27)
**VOX, VOCIS** – L – voice (87)

## GREEK ROOT WORDS

**AGON** – G. – contest, struggle (44)
**AKROS** – G. – topmost, high point, (74)
**AMPHI** – G. – both (12)
**ANA** – G. – up, back again (76)
**ANTHROPOS** – G. – man, mankind (26)
**ARCHOS** – G. – lead, rule, be first, begin (17)
**ATHLON** – G. – prize, award (43)
**BARBAROS** – G. – foreign (98)
**DERMA** – G. – skin, hide (39)
**DOKEIN** – G. – think, have an opinion (100)
**DROMOS** – G. – race course, running (45)
**ELEKTRON** – G. – amber (71)
**ERGON** – G. – work (95)
**EU** – G. – well, good (14)
**HETEROS** – G. – other, different (54)
**HIPPOS** – G. – horse (6)
**HOLOS** – G. – whole, entire, complete (36)
**HOMOS** – G. – same (53)
**HYPER** – G. – above, overly, beyond (80)
**HYPO** – G. – under, below (81)
**IATROS** – G. – physician, comforter (33)
**KATA** – G. – down, against, completely (75)
**KYKLOS** – G. – ring, circle, wheel (20)
**LEON** – G. – lion (3)
**MONOS** – G. – alone, solitary (92)
**NAUS** – G. – ship, boat (51)
**ORNIS** – G. – bird (8)
**ORTHOS** – G. – straight, correct (99)
**PAIS, PAIDOS** – G. – child (30)
**PERI** – G. – around (21)
**RHINOS** – G. – nose, snout (37)
**SCHOLE** – G. – leisure, free time (31)
**THEOS** – G. – god (22)

© 2003 J&J Lundquist

# PRONOUNCING LATIN WORDS

Pronouncing Latin words is EASY compared to pronouncing English words. Latin is so predictable and regular that when you learn a few rules, you can hardly go wrong. Most beginning Latin books devote a page and a half to explaining how to pronounce vowels, diphthongs (two-letter vowel sounds), and consonants, and then the new Latin students are off and running!

## VOWELS

Long
a – ah – as in f<u>a</u>ther
e – ay – as in ob<u>ey</u>
i – ee – as in mach<u>i</u>ne
o – oh – as in n<u>o</u>te
u – oo – as in r<u>u</u>le (not pupil)

Short
a – uh – as in ide<u>a</u>
e – eh – as in b<u>e</u>t
i – i – as in b<u>i</u>t
o – ah – as in pot
u – oo – as in book

## DIPHTHONGS

You need to know that a Latin word has as many syllables as it contains vowels – or diphthongs. Doubled vowels are pronounced separately, so the sord "SUUS" (SOO-OOS) has two syllables. Diphthongs, on the other hand, are two vowel sounds which are said so quickly together that they make only one sound and therefore only one syllable.

ae (ah-ay) as in aisle
au (ah-oo) as in found
ei (ay-ee) as in neighbor
eu (ay-oo) said as one syllable (no English equivalent)
oe (oh-ay) as in boy
ui (oo-ee) as in queen

## CONSONANTS

c as in cat – never soft as in cent or city
g as in go – never soft as in gentle
s as in sit – never as in noise
t as in tea – never "sh" as in nation
v = w as in win
x = "ks" as in tax, never "gs" as in exam
ch, ph, th – ignore the "h" and pronounce as c, p, t.

Before you begin, why not turn to the Pronunciation Guide (pp. xvi & xvii) and say the words softly to yourself for practice. Accent falls on the first syllable of a two-syllable word. In a longer word, the accent falls on the next to the last syllable if it is long. If that syllable is short, the one just preceding it is accented. E.G. – annus (AH noos); discipulus (dis SKEE poo loos).

# PRONUNCIATION GUIDE

## by Nora MacDonald

*Nora MacDonald has been teaching Latin at Roosevelt High School in Seattle, Washington since 1977, when she replaced her Latin teacher, Miss Gail Ingle. She holds both a B.A. and an M.A. in Latin from the University of Washington. She won an NEH award to study Plutarch at the University of Kentucky in the summer of 1993. In May of 1999, she received Washington State's Sharon Christa McAuliffe Award for Excellence.*

*Mrs. MacDonald continues to promote the study of Latin through the American Classical League and the National Junior Classical League, for which she served as Washington State Chairman from 1984-1994. She has led eight student tours to Italy and has been a sponsor for her students at 25 National Junior Classical League conventions. She recently completed a five-year term as NJCL Graphic Arts Contest Coordinator for the 1500-1700 delegates who annually attend the summer competition.*

\* \* \* \* \* \* \* \* \*

Please refer to "Pronouncing Latin Words" (p.xv) and study the EASY and REGULAR rules! As you see, the sounds of letters in Latin and Greek were constant. You will notice that the pronunciation guide on this page for some of the roots (particularly some of the Greek roots) will seem unfamiliar at first. Whenever the English pronunciation of the root has tended to supersede the ancient Greek, *the more common alternate will appear in parentheses beside the correct ancient pronunciation.*

One important point: Because we have not used dictionary diacritical marks in this guide, and because long "o" is difficult to distinguish from its short counterpart, long "o" will be written "oh" and short "o" will be followed by a double consonant as in "loss." Please remember that "s" is always soft (as in "set") and "g" is always hard (as in "get"). And, finally, "ph" and "th" (which appear rarely in this guide) will follow the English pronunciation in "photograph" and "theater." Now you are free to go placidly among the words. Pax vobiscum!

1 – **CANIS** – KAH nis
2 – **FELES, FELIS** – FAY les, FAY lis
3 – **LEON** – LAY ohn
4 – **EQUUS** – EH kwoos
5 – **CABALLUS** – cah BAHL loos
6 – **HIPPOS** – HIP poss
7 – **PORCUS** – POR koos
8 – **ORNIS** – OR nis
9 – **AVIS** – AH wis
10 – **GREX, GREGIS** – GREKS, GRE gis
11 – **OMNIS** – OHM nis
12 – **AMPHI** – AHM pee (AHM fee)
13 – **AMBI** – AHM bee
14 – **EU** – EH oo
15 – **MALUS** – MAH loos
16 – **E, EX** – AY, EKS
17 – **ARCHOS** – AHR koss
18 – **ARCUS** – AHR koos
19 – **CIRCUM** – KEER coom

20 – **KYKLOS** – KOOK loss (KIK loss)
21 – **PERI** – PEH ree
22 – **THEOS** – TAY oss
23 – **DEUS** – DAY oos
24 – **DIVINUS** – dee WEE noos
25 – **HOMO, HOMINIS** – HOH moh, HOH mi nis
26 – **ANTHROPOS** – AHN troh poss
27 – **VIR** – WEER
28 – **FEMINA** – FAY mi nah
29 – **INFANS, INFANTIS** – EEN fahns, een FAHN tis
30 – **PAIS, PAIDOS** – pah EES, peye DOSS
31 – **SCHOLE** – SKOH lay
32 – **LUDO, LUSUS** – LOO doh, LOO soos
33 – **IATROS** – yah TROSS
34 – **MEDICUS** – MEH di koos
35 – **SANUS** – SAH noos
36 – **HOLOS** – HOH loss
37 – **RHINOS** – HREE noss (REYE noss)
38 – **CORNU** – KOR noo

© 2003 Nora MacDonald

39 – **DERMA** – DAIR mah (DER mah)
40 – **CUTIS** – KOO tis
41 – **COR, CORDIS** – KOR, KOR dis
42 – **DORSUM** – DOR soom
43 – **ATHLON** – AHT lohn
44 – **AGON** – AH gohn
45 – **DROMOS** – DROH moss
46 – **MONS, MONTIS** – MOHNS, MOHN tis
47 – **HUMUS** – HOO moos
48 – **FOLIUM** – FOH lee oom
49 – **SAL, SALIS** – SAHL, SAH lis
50 – **MARE** – MAH reh
51 – **NAUS** – NAH oos
52 – **NAVIS** – NAH wis
53 – **HOMOS** – HOH moss
54 – **HETEROS** – HEH teh ross
55 – **CARDO, CARDINIS** – KAR doh, KAR di nis
56 – **PORTA** – POR tah
57 – **PORTO, PORTATUM** – POR toh, por TAH toom
58 – **NOVUS** – NOH woos
59 – **ORDO, ORDINIS** – OR doh, OR din is
60 – **SAECULUM** – SEYE koo loom
61 – **PRIMUS** – PREE moos
62 – **SECUNDUS** – seh KOON doos
63 – **TERTIUS** – TAIR tee oos
64 – **QUARTUS** – KWAR toos
65 – **QUINTUS** – KWEEN toos
66 – **SEXTUS** – SEX toos
67 – **SEPTIMUS** – SEP ti moos
68 – **OCTAVUS** – ohk TAH woos
69 – **NONUS** – NOH noos
70 – **DECIMUS** – DEH ki moos
71 – **ELECTRON** – eh LEK trohn

72 – **GRADUS** – GRAH doos
73 – **PLUS, PLURIS** – PLOOS, PLOO ris
74 – **AKROS** – AH kross
75 – **KATA** – KAH tah
76 – **ANA** – AH nah
77 – **DUCO, DUCTUM** – DOO koh, DOOK toom
78 – **AGO, ACTUM** – AH goh, AHK toom
79 – **PENDO, PENSUM** – PEN doh, PAIN soom
80 – **HYPER** – HOO pair, (HEYE purr)
81 – **HYPO** – HOO poh, (HEYE poh)
82 – **SUPER** – SOO pair
83 – **SUB** – SOOB
84 – **RUMPO, RUPTUM** – ROOM poh, ROOP toom
85 – **PAX, PACIS** – PAHKS, PAH kiss
86 – **SPECTO, SPECTATUM** – SPEK toh, spek TAH toom
87 – **VOX, VOCIS** – WOHKS, WO kiss
88 – **LOQUOR, LOCUTUS** – LOH kwor, loh KOO toos
89 – **FELIX, FELICIS** – FAY leeks, fay LEE kis
90 – **FIDES** – FIH days
91 – **SOLUS** – SOH loos
92 – **MONOS** – MOH noss
93 – **RIDEO, RISUM** – REE day oh, REE soom
94 – **LABORO, LABORATUM** – lah BOH roh, lah boh RAH toom
95 – **ERGON** – AIR gohn
96 – **DURUS** – DOO roos
97 – **BELLUM** – BEL loom
98 – **BARBAROS** – BAR bah ross
99 – **ORTHOS** – OR toss, (OR thoss)
100 – **DOKEIN** – DOH kayn

© 2003 Nora MacDonald

# THE EIGHT PARTS OF SPEECH

*By Nora MacDonald*

1. A **noun** is the name of a person, place, thing, quality, or idea.
   Examples: Mr. Rogers, Euro-Disney, computer, happiness, bureaucracy.

2. A **pronoun** is a word which takes the place of a noun.
   Examples: he, she, it, me, you, I, anyone, someone, who, whom.

3. A **verb** is a word that shows an action, occurrence, or state of being.

    A **transitive verb** always has an object:
      Some marmots **like** mountains.
    An **intransitive verb** has no object:
      Some marmots **live** in the mountains.
    The **active voice** shows the subject performs the action.
      Joe **eats** seaweed.
    The **passive voice** shows the subject receives the action.
      The seaweed **is eaten** by Joe.
    The words be, seem, and appear are called **linking verbs**. This verb shows no action and acts as an = sign between subject and predicate.

4. An **adverb** tells how, when, where, why, and how much or to what extent. It modifies a verb, adjective, adverb or preposition.
   Examples: radically, tomorrow, there, slightly, very, bravely.

5. An **adjective** denotes color, size or quality. It answers which, what kind of, and how many. It modifies a noun or pronoun. In Latin it will always agree with the word it modifies in case, number, or gender.
   Examples: orange, miniscule, dazzling

6. A **conjunction** connects words, phrases, or clauses.
   Examples: and, but, or, because.

7. A **preposition** shows the relationship of its object to other words in the sentence. It combines with a noun or pronoun to add meaning to a sentence. A prepositional phrase can often be left out of the sentence and the sentence will stand on its own.
   Examples: I wish to travel **around** the world. Around is the preposition. World is its object.

8. An **interjection** expresses strong feeling.
   Examples: Oh! Yea!

# ROMAN NUMERALS

Along with children's early lessons in arithmetic, it is enjoyable to teach the Latin words for numbers – both cardinal (UNUS – one) and ordinal (PRIMUS – first). We have so many English words which are based on these fertile roots that it is immediately clear to anyone how profitable it is to make the effort to learn them! But before you begin on the words, it is GREAT FUN to learn the ROMAN NUMERALS.

We introduced DIGITUS in *Volume I* (p. 26) for a special reason. In Latin it meant both "finger" and "number." The ancient folks counted on their fingers, so when they wanted to write numbers down, it was natural to DRAW fingers to show how many! I, II, III, etc. When they came to "four" (4), at first they just used four ones (IIII). But when human beings have to deal with more than THREE of something, it's hard to see at a glance exactly how many things there are without counting. SO THE ROMANS DID A VERY CLEVER THING! They had five fingers on each hand to work with, just as we do, and they could see that FIVE fingers (IIIII) would only add to the confusion! How to picture the WHOLE HAND?

Drawing all the fingers held up together resulted in a kind of blobby "mitten" effect. But, by holding the THUMB away from the fingers and drawing the shape between, they came up with FIVE - "V"! And for two hands full of fingers, they turned one V upside down and wrote TEN – "X"! (WOULDN'T YOU BE PROUD IF YOU HAD THOUGHT OF IT?) They still weren't quite happy with IIII, though. Now that they had such a good FIVE – "V" – someone said "We'll write one (I) first and then (V) to say 'one less than five'!" (IV)

"AND," chimed in another clever Roman, "well write five first and then one (VI) after it to say 'five and one more' when we mean SIX!" This made everyone happy! THEY HAD BUILT A NUMBER SYSTEM WITH THEIR TWO BARE HANDS!

| | |
|---|---|
| 1 – I | 6 – VI |
| 2 – II | 7 – VII |
| 3 – III | 8 – VIII |
| 4 – IV | 9 – IX |
| 5 – V | 10 – X |

They could count as high as they pleased with this system. A smaller number before a larger one meant SUBTRACT. A smaller number after a larger one meant ADD. All they needed were some more symbols for 50 (L), 100 (C), 500 (D), and 1000 (M). Now they could figure out any large number – even the dates of famous events in history! Would your children like to figure these out?

The Norman invasion of Britain – MLXVI (M LX VI) = 1066
Columbus discovers America – MCDXCII (M CD XC II) = 1492
America declares independence – MDCCLXXVI (M DCC LXX VI) 1776

©2003 Joégil K. Lundquist

# THE GREEK ALPHABET

| Capital | Lower Case | Name of Letter | Sound of Letter |
|---|---|---|---|
| A | α | alpha | a as in father |
| B | β | beta | b as in boy |
| Γ | γ | gamma | g as in go |
| Δ | δ | delta | d as in did |
| E | ε | epsilon | ĕ as in get |
| Z | ζ | zeta | dz as in adze |
| H | η | eta | ē as in they |
| Θ | θ | theta | th as in theater |
| I | ι | iota | ĭ as in tin / ī as in machine |
| K | κ | kappa | k as in kite |
| Λ | λ | lambda | l as in late |
| M | μ | mu | m as in mate |
| N | ν | nu | n as in not |
| Ξ | ξ | xi | x as in tax |
| O | ο | omicron | ŏ as in obey |
| Π | π | pi | p as in pay |
| P | ρ | rho | r as in rheostat |
| Σ | σς | sigma | s as in system |
| T | τ | tau | t as in take |
| Υ | υ | upsilon | French u or German ü |
| Φ | φ | phi | ph as in phone |
| X | χ | chi | German ch as in Bach |
| Ψ | ψ | psi | ps as in lapse |
| Ω | ω | omega | ō as in go |

Reprinted with the permission of The American Classical League

This page is available as a colorful poster (19" x 24½") from The American Classical League, Miami University, Oxford, Ohio 45056.

# canis

**[KAH nis]   dog**

canine – *n.* a dog; *adj.* dog-like
caninity – canine quality or trait; dog-like nature
canine teeth – extra long, pointed teeth used for tearing
*Canidae* – the family of dog-like carnivorous mammals including dogs, wolves, jackals, foxes, coyotes, and hyenas
Canis Major – "Great Dog," a constellation in the shape of a dog
Canicula – Sirius, the "Dog Star," the brightest star in the constellation Canis Major

**TEACHING NOTES:** Dogs were the first animals to be tamed by man. The Greeks raised large lion-hunting dogs called mastiffs. The Romans kept dogs as pets, as hunting dogs, and as sheepherders. Evidence of a pet dog was found in almost every large garden excavated in Pompeii. One house had a floor mosaic of a dog at the entry with the warning "**Cave Canem**" (pronounced *CAH-way CAH-nem*) "Beware of the dog." Today, the police **CANINE** unit (abbreviated as K-9) includes dogs who help officers by using their keen sense of smell to find people and illegal substances.

In humans, the **CANINE** teeth (sometimes called eyeteeth) are the third pair of teeth from the front of each side of the upper and lower jaw. Each student can identify his or her own canine teeth and those of a friend. Perhaps a student will want to research the different uses of the incisors, bicuspids, and molars, as well as **CANINES**, and report to the rest of the class.

**CANIS MAJOR** is the companion constellation to Orion, the hunter. The three stars that make up Orion's belt point southeast to Sirius, which is the brightest star in the chest of the Great Dog. Sirius is brighter than our sun, but it is so far away that it takes nine years for its light to reach Earth. Procyon comes from Latin *pro*-before and Greek *kyon*-dog. Sometimes called the "Little Dog Star," Procyon is a first-magnitude star in the constellation **CANIS MINOR** or the "Little Dog." Procyon got its name because the Greeks noticed that it rose before the Dog Star. Procyon forms a triangle with Betelgeuse, in Orion's right shoulder, and Sirius in **CANIS MAJOR**. A book with pictures of constellations is a valuable aid for searching the night sky and learning to identify these dot-to-dot pictures in the sky!

© 2003 J&J Lundquist

LATIN

# feles

**[FAY les, FAY lis]   cat**

feline – *n.* a cat; *adj.* cat-like
felinity – cat-like disposition
felinophilia (philia G. - love, Vol. I, p. 6) – love for cats
felinophobia (phobos G. - fear, Vol. I, p. 7) – fear of cats
*Felidae* – the whole cat tribe, large and small, including domestic cats, lions, tigers, leopards, cheetahs, lynxes, panthers, cougars, etc.

**TEACHING NOTES:** Domestic cats were not as popular in ancient Rome as were dogs, although some were found in Pompeii, buried in the volcanic ash of Mt. Vesuvius. There is a mosaic picture of a cat in one of the excavated houses. When the Romans used the word **FELES**, they thought of lions or wild cats. However, they referred to small domestic cats as *feles catus*. **CATUS** means shrewd, intelligent, and sly, which certainly describes the character of most cats.

Teaching this word **FELES** provides a wonderful occasion to introduce the concept of scientific classification. *The World Book Encyclopedia* says that early man divided all animals into just two classifications: "useful" and "harmful." The Greek philosopher and teacher Aristotle devised a way of classifying the relatively few animals that he knew about, but it was a Swedish naturalist in the 18th century, Karl von Linne, who gave us the present system of seven levels of classification: Kingdom, Phylum, Class, Order, Family, Genus, and Species.

Our pet cats belong to the Kingdom *Animalia*; the Phylum *Chordata* (having backbones); the Class *Mammalia* (nursing their young); the Order *Carnivora* (meat-eating); the Family *Felidae*; the Genus *Feles*; and the Species *Feles Catus*. Karl von Linne was known as Carolus Linneaus because he wrote his books in Latin so that scholars all over the world would be able to identify animals by using the same names. In those days ALL real scholars knew Latin!

© 2003 J&J Lundquist

GREEK

λεων

# leon

### [LAY on]   lion

lion – the largest member of the cat family *Felidae*
lioness – a female lion
leonine – lion-like
dandelion (dens L. - tooth) – weedy plant with deeply toothed leaves and golden-yellow tufted flower
chameleon (chamai G. - on the ground) – a lizard with a large head able to change color for protection
leopard (pardos G. - black leopard) – tawny panther with black spots
Leo – the constellation of the Lion; zodiac sign; a boy's name
lionize – to treat as an object of great interest or importance
lion's share – the biggest and best portion of anything

**TEACHING NOTES:** From earliest times, the **LION** has been known as the "king of beasts." Known for their strength, courage, and fearsome hunting ability, **LIONS** inspired men from all eras in history to call themselves "**LIONS**." *The Bible* mentions "the **LION** of the tribe of Judah" (Rev. 5:5). In the time of the Crusades, the English king was called "Richard the **LION**-Hearted." Thirteen Popes have been named **LEO**, and **LEON**, **LEONARD**, and **LEONARDO** are popular boy's names even today. In the animal kingdom, **LIONS** seem quite civilized, living in family communities called prides, perhaps because the members, cared for and protected, are "proud" of each other! The adult male **LION** is the only cat with a mane, which makes him look larger and more formidable both to his enemies and to his prey. His job is to protect the pride and its territory from intruders. The female **LIONESS** does the hunting for food so all in the pride may eat. She brings home antelope and other large animals to share with the cubs and other **LIONESSES**. Of course the largest male gets "the **LION'S SHARE**."

**DANDELIONS** (*dent de lion* - French - "tooth of the lion") have pointed leaves which may have resembled a lion's fangs to some early naturalist, but even more, the brilliant, tufted, yellow flower seems to suggest a lion's mane. The green part of the plant is edible but it is rarely prized because it has a habit of invading grassy lawns where it is not wanted.

The **CHAMELEON** is a small lizard with a large head known for its ability to change color. The head is defined from the rest of the body by a crest of bone called a casque which resembles a lion's mane. Perhaps the ancients thought they saw a tiny tawny lion on the brown ground!

© 2003 J&J Lundquist

LATIN

# equus

**[EH kwoos]  horse**

*Equidae* – scientific term for the horse family

equestrian – a person skilled in horse riding; pertaining to horseback riding

equine – of, pertaining to, or resembling a horse

equestrienne – feminine form; a horsewoman; female equestrian

**TEACHING NOTES:** The use of Latin terms in scientific classification began long ago so that biologists and other scientists could talk to each other no matter their native language. In scientific classification, ***EQUIDAE***, the horse family, includes horses, donkeys, mules, zebras, and some extinct "ungulates" (animals having hooves). The horse we know and love belongs to the Kingdom *Animalia,* Phylum *Chordata* (having backbones)*,* Class *Mammalia* (nursing the young), Order *Herbivora Ungulata* (eating grass or other plants and having hooves), Family *EQUIDAE,* Genus ***EQUUS***, Species ***EQUUS*** *Caballus*.

The history of the horse family, or ***EQUIDAE***, is interesting. The horse is native to all continents except Australia. Fossils have shown that in the Ice Age horses roamed all over North and South America, but then, unaccountably, they disappeared. They were later reintroduced by man to the Western Hemisphere and to Australia where they have thrived ever since.

Our word "horse" is from the Anglo Saxon *hors*. However, most of our words relating to horses are derivatives from the Latin **EQUUS** or the Greek **HIPPOS**. The Romans called the domesticated horse **EQUUS CABALLUS** or simply **CABALLUS** (as they shortened **Feles Catus** to simply *"catus"* or *"cat"*), which then became the source for derivatives in Spanish (*caballo* - horse, *caballero* - horseman); in French (*cheval* - horse, *cavalier* or *chevalier* - horseman); and Italian (*cavallo* - horse).

Some have erroneously assumed that **EQUERRY** (meaning the stables belonging to a princely household; the body of officers in charge of the stables) is a derivative from **EQUUS**. It is not. It is from the middle Latin word *scuria* meaning stable.

© 2003 J&J Lundquist

LATIN

# caballus

**[cah BAHL loos]    horse**

cavalry – a division of an army in which the soldiers ride horses
*cheval* – (*French*) horse
chivalry – a code of courteous conduct which was followed by knights
    (horsemen) of the Middle Ages
*caballo* – (*Spanish*) horse
*cavallo* – (*Italian*) horse
*chevalet* – (*French* - little horse) the bridge on a stringed musical
    instrument, as a violin; any wooden frame for holding or sup-
    porting something; equiv. to *cheval* - horse
cavalcade – procession of riders on horseback, or in carriages
Chevalier, (Maurice) – French actor and singer

**TEACHING NOTES:**   The derivatives of this Latin word, **CABALLO**, are a beautiful example of spelling pronunciation (spelling a word the way it is spoken, rather than pronouncing it the way it is spelled). They show the changes in spelling that can occur according to the way people of different countries pronounce words. The Greeks pronounced their *b* (beta) as though it were the letter *v*, and they still do. The Spanish, who originally spoke a dialect of Latin, retained the "b" spelling in **CABALLO**, but their pronunciation of the letter is very soft and sounds more like a *v* to us than the bombastic *b* sounds we use in English. The French and Italians simply changed the letter *b* to a *v* in their derivative words.

　　The concept of **CHIVALRY** came from Latin through Old French into English; hence the French spelling and pronunciation of "ch" at the beginning of the word and, of course, in **Maurice Chevalier's** name (the horseman, the knight), a wonderful name for an actor who always played such **CHIVALROUS** characters.

　　The French word **CHEVALET** is a diminutive of their word **CHEVAL**. It described as a "little horse" the bridge on a violin, cello, or bass viol. **CHEVALET** also is used to describe the wooden trestles supporting a bridge and even a sawhorse used in a carpenter's shop.

　　A **CAVALCADE** was originally a parade of riders on horseback or horse drawn carriages, but it can be any long procession of vehicles or people or even ships. It is sometimes used to refer to the progression of historical events through decades or centuries.

© 2003 J&J Lundquist

# hippos

**GREEK**
ἱππος

### [HIP poss]   horse

hippopotamus (potamos G. - river) – river horse
hippodrome (dromos G. - race course) – horse race track
hippocampus (kampos G. - sea monster) – sea horse
hippology (logos G. - word, study, Vol. I, p. 15) – study of horses
hippophile (philia G. - love, Vol. I, p. 6) – one who loves horses
Eohippus (eo G. - dawn) – dawn horse, a small extinct horse
hippiatric (iatros G. - healer) – pertaining to treating the diseases of horses
Hippotigris (tigris G. - tiger) – a subgenus of the *Equidae* family, including zebras

**TEACHING NOTES:** A **HIPPOPOTAMUS** is a four-toed herbivorous mammal, able to remain underwater for extended periods, which lives in African rivers and estuaries (where a river meets the sea). A **HIPPODROME** for the Greeks was a large open stadium where chariot races were held. **HIPPOCAMPUS** refers to the curious, little, tube-nosed creatures we know as sea horses. In Greek mythology, Neptune, the God of the Sea, drove a chariot pulled by a fantastic creature also called **HIPPOCAMPUS**, with the body of a horse and the tail of a dolphin.

Philippos was a man's name in ancient Greece (a combined form of *philos* and *hippos*), so the name *Philip* means a man who loves horses. **EOHIPPUS**, the earliest known species of the *Equidae* family, was a little, four-toed fellow who lived in the Eocene Era 65 million years ago. The U. S. Postal Service gave us a stamp with his picture on it a few years ago.

Scientists must have had fun coming up with the genus name of **HIPPOTIGRIS** (a horse with the markings of a tiger) for zebras. It might be a challenge to put the word **HIPPOTIGRIS** on the chalkboard and see if students can guess what kind of animal it is before giving them the definition. This can bring home the point that knowledge of Greek and Latin still plays a vital role in the sciences today and can help students figure out the meaning of words they don't already know.

© 2003 J&J Lundquist

LATIN

# porcus

**[POR koos]     pig, hog, swine**

pork – meat from a pig
porcine – pig-like, fat, lazy
porcupine (spina L. - thorn) – spiny or prickly pig-shaped rodent
porpoise (porcus piscis L. - pig fish) – a blunt, snouted, aquatic mammal, similar to a dolphin
pork barrel – barrel in which salt pork is stored
porker – a young pig raised for food
"pork" – money for local projects from the public "trough"
porcelain – a fine, white earthenware noted for its translucence and transparent glaze; china

**TEACHING NOTES:** Considering what they have contributed to the well-being of mankind for the past 8,000 years or so, pigs, hogs, boars (swine in general) get precious little respect! It is always an insult to call anyone a "pig." It would be interesting to have a class discussion to consider the reasons why and to think about how pigs are portrayed in literature. Even the film *Babe* presents an endearing pig who longs to be a dog! The cat tells Babe that pigs are given homes and fed only so they can finally be eaten! Since ancient times, pigs were raised for food and other uses. Every part of a pig is useful. An encyclopedia or the Internet will tell you of all the products we depend upon which come from pigs. Any fans of American football in class? Did you know that footballs were originally made out of a pig's hide? Former football players may refer to the years they played football as their *"pigskin"* days. Referring to a football as a *pigskin* usually indicates a feeling of affection and nostalgia for the game.

Before the days of refrigeration, **PORK** meat was preserved by packing it in salt and storing this valuable food in barrels for a family's year-round sustenance. By metaphor, the state or national treasuries came to be referred to as "**PORK BARRELS**." Even today, legislators and congressmen who want the treasury to pay for projects in their own districts help each other by voting for each other's local projects out of the public treasury, calling the projects "**PORK**."

What do **PORCELAIN** and pigs have in common? The word **PORCELAIN** came from the Latin *porcellus* (the diminutive of **PORCUS** - meaning *"little pig"*) via Old French *"porcelaine"* and Italian *"porcellana"* which was a cowrie shell, so named because the shape of the shell resembled a pig's back. When European merchants brought back samples of Chinese **PORCELAIN**, the fine white surface of the earthenware resembled the inner white surface of the shell and the china became known as **PORCELAIN**.

© 2003 J&J Lundquist

GREEK

ορνις

# ornis ornithos

### [OR nis]   bird

**ornithology** (<u>logos</u> G. - word, study, Vol. I, p. 15) – study of the nature and habits of birds

**ornithivorous** (<u>vorare</u> L. - devour, swallow up) – bird-eating

**ornithopterous** (<u>pteron</u> G. - wing) – having wings like a bird

**ornithotrophe** (<u>trophos</u> G. - feeder) – place to feed and observe birds

**ornithocephalic** (<u>kephale</u> G. - head) – having a head shaped like a bird's

**ornithopter** (<u>pteron</u> G. - wing) – machine designed to fly by flapping wings

**ornithophile** (<u>philia</u> G. - love, Vol. I, p. 6) – lover of birds

**ornithomancy** (<u>mantis</u> G. - diviner, prophet) – telling fortunes by observing birds

**TEACHING NOTES:** This Greek word **ORNIS** gives us a whole collection of words which are great fun to learn and practice before the next visit to the aviary (bird house) at the zoo! *The Oxford English Dictionary* provides many more of them than we can introduce here, but we encourage you to explore more of them in the biggest dictionary you can find. Help children to become amateur **ORNITHOLOGISTS** by giving them a list of birds in your local area, showing them pictures so they can identify them, and giving them a journal to record their sightings. It could lead to a lifetime of pleasureable bird watching with fellow enthusiasts all over the world.

    **ORNITH** combines with some of our old friends from Volume I (**logos** and **philia**) and partners with new ones (**kephalos**) to yield words like **ORNITHOCEPHALIC** (or-nith-o-CEPH-a-lic) – "bird-head." The Greek word is spelled with a kappa which is a hard "k" sound. The English derivative changes the k to c. In English, remember, c followed by e, i, or y is pronounced like "s." Try saying **ORNITHOCEPHALIC** several times until you are sure you own it! We can hear the poet Emily Dickinson saying, "Now there's a word to lift your hat to!" **ORNITHOMANCY** - Many ancient people thought they could foretell the future by watching birds.

    **ORNITHOMANCY** was an ancient practice of trying to foretell the future by watching birds. While birds probably don't have any supernatural information, we can learn much from observing their behaviors and migration patterns. See the Audubon Society on the Internet at *www.audubon.org*.

© 2003 J&J Lundquist

LATIN

# avis

**[AH wis]   bird**

aviary – a large building in which birds are kept

aviate – to navigate the air in an airplane; to fly

aviation – aerial navigation by means of an airplane; the science of powered flight; design and development of aircraft

aviator – pilot of an airplane

avian – of or pertaining to birds

aviculture (cultura L. - tilling, raising) – the raising of and caring for birds, especially wild birds in captivity

**TEACHING NOTES:** Imitation is the sincerest form of flattery. Man, admiring the freedom of birds, has always wanted to **AVIATE**, or fly. Some of the most creative inventors have tried to make it possible. A favorite Greek myth tells about Daedalus and his son, Icarus. King Minos of Crete hired the architect, Daedalus, to design a labyrinth in which to keep the monstrous Minotaur. Minos later imprisoned Daedalus, who escaped by designing wings for Icarus and himself. He made them from feathers and wax, and they worked well until foolish Icarus, ignoring his father's warning, flew too high. The sun melted the wax and Icarus fell into the sea and drowned. So much for feathers and wax! Man had to go back to the drawing board! But **AVIATION** was an ongoing aspiration of man.

Leonardo da Vinci, the great Renaissance painter and inventor, designed a flying machine which he called an **ornithopter** (see p. 8) based on the concept of mechanically flapping wings, but it never actually flew. Although balloonists and others tried, human flying never really got off the ground until the Wright brothers, Orville and Wilbur, flew their first airplane at Kitty Hawk, North Carolina, on December 17, 1903. They were mankind's first real **AVIATORS**.

It's interesting to note that most of the derivative words pertaining to man's aviation technology have come from the Latin word **AVIS**, and most of the words concerning the study of the birds themselves have come from the Greek word **ORNIS**. The Greeks excelled in philosophy and scientific study of the world around them. The Romans were builders and engineers. How fortunate we are to be the heirs of both of these rich cultural legacies.

**NEW WORD:** **avitite** – (Don't look for this one in the dictionary! We made it up!) Our definition: What one has who feels ready to eat the bird to be served on Thanksgiving Day!

© 2003 J&J Lundquist

LATIN

# grex
# gregis

**[GREKS, GRE gis]**
**flock, herd, drove, group, troop, company**

gregarious – living in herds, flocks, or social groups; fond of company, socially outgoing and friendly

egregious (e, ex L. - out, away) – out of the herd; outstandingly bad

congregate (cum L. - together, Vol. I, p. 23) – gather together as a group

congregation – a flock of churchgoers gathered together for worship with a cleric as shepherd

segregate (se L. - apart) – to separate from the group

aggregate (ad L. - to, Vol. I, p. 20) – to gather together in a lump or sum

**TEACHING NOTES:** Our vocabulary has evolved naturally and steadily from the conscious experience of humankind on planet Earth. Men and animals have always tended to **CONGREGATE** – to gather together in groups for support and protection. When a human or animal acts in a mean or destructive way, the group considers the behavior **EGREGIOUS**. (Who has committed **EGREGIOUS** acts in history?) The herd, the group, the company of one's own kind, is comforting and tends to encourage behaviors which promote well-being and progress. It is valuable to study the different societies that are found in the world today and to try to understand why they behave in very different ways toward each other as well as toward other societies in the rest of the world. We couldn't find it in the dictionary, but we'd like to offer **GREXOLOGY** as a suitable term for this study of groups. Do you like it?

It is valuable, too, to study the behavior of animals in their herds and flocks and to see how man has adopted some of the flock or "herd-like" thinking to guide human behavior in society. Some animals are known to **SEGREGATE** or abandon injured, diseased, or merely "different" members of the group, fearing that they may endanger the group as a whole. Others have been known to protect such disadvantaged flock members at the risk of their own lives. The word **EGREGIOUS** once meant remarkable, excellent, distinguished, or renowned and was a term of admiration. **EGREGIOUS**, in more recent times, is used to describe behavior or actions which are very bad, gross, flagrant, or outrageous. Times change and so do the standards of group behavior and how words are used to describe it.

© 2003 J&J Lundquist

LATIN

# omnis

### [OHM nis]   each, every, all

**omnipotence** (<u>potens</u> L. - powerful, able) – all power
**omnipotent** – all powerful
**omnipresent** (<u>praesens</u> L. - present) – present everywhere
**omniscience** (<u>scire</u> L. - to know, Vol. I, p. 97) – knowledge of all
**omniscient** – all knowing
**omnivorous** (<u>vorare</u> L. - to eat greedily; swallow) – willing to eat anything and everything
**omnibus** – vehicle capable of carrying many passengers
**omnidirectional** (<u>dirigere</u> L. - direct, guide) – capable of transmitting or receiving radio waves from all directions

**TEACHING NOTES:**  In Volume I, page 25, (JUNGO, JUNCTUM) we discussed the *conjugations* of Latin verbs in which endings are joined to the basic stem of the verb to tell **who** ( I, you, he, she, it, we, you, they) is doing the action, and **when**, whether it is present, past, or future.

Nouns and the adjectives which modify them are *declined*. That means that endings are tacked on to the basic stem of the noun or adjective which will tell you whether the noun is: **1 - the subject** of the sentence (the person doing the action); **2 - a possessor or owner** (where we would use **'s**); **3 - indirect object** (to or for the noun); **4 - direct object** or receiver of the action; **5 - object of a preposition** such as by, in, or with. Here's how **declining** works with **OMNIS**.

    1. **Nominative** case - **All** are running. "**Omnes** currunt."
    2. **Genitive** (possessive) case - **Everyone's** shirts are green. "Tunicae **omnis** virides sunt."
    3. **Dative** case - There are prizes **for everyone**. "Sunt palmae **omnibus**."
    4. **Accusative** case - The rain soaked **everybody**. "Pluvia **omnes** madefaciebat."
    5. **Ablative** case - Dogs are running **with everybody**. "Canes cum **omnibus** currunt."

Back in about 1828, the French built a vehicle which was long enough to carry several passengers and called it a "voiture OMNIBUS"- *vehicle for all*. The next year the English built two similar ones which ran from Paddington to the city of London—known ever after as simply "the bus." So the word we use today is simply the last syllable of the dative and ablative case endings for the Latin word OMNIBUS.

© 2003 J&J Lundquist

GREEK

αμφι

# amphi

**[AHM pee, AHM fee]    both**

amphitheater (<u>theatron</u> G. - place for seeing) – theater with audience on both sides of the central stage area

amphibian (<u>bios</u> G. - life, Vol. I, p. 73) – animal, including frogs, toads, newts, and salamanders, which can live and breathe both in water and on land

amphora (<u>pherein</u> G. - to carry) – a large jar or jug with handles on both sides for carrying liquids

amphoric sound – a sound made by blowing across the mouth of a bottle or jug

amphigory (<u>guros</u> G. - circle) – a story or rhyme with opposite statements resulting in nonsense

**TEACHING NOTES:** An **AMPHITHEATER**, the predecessor of our modern sports stadiums, were large arenas with lots of seating on all sides of a central oval performance or competition area. The Colosseum in Rome is an **AMPHITHEATER** where Romans went to be entertained by gladiators who fought each other or opposed wild animals.

In ancient Greece an **AMPHORA** was a large, heavy jar used for transporting liquids such as wine, oil, and water. The potters put handles on both sides of the jug so two people could carry it. It tapered down to a point at the bottom so it could sit in a hole in uneven ground or be wedged among rocks. It was set into a hole in a board or stone slab when it was loaded onto a ship or stored in a shop or kitchen. Smaller **AMPHORAE** (plural form) were filled with sacred oil and given as prizes to winners of games at festivals. These were molded with disk-shaped bases so they could stand alone on a flat surface. The shape of these prizes is often imitated in the trophy cups awarded at athletic contests today. If clay is available, it would be fun for students to make some small **AMPHORAE** and then fire and decorate them.

To make **AMPHORIC SOUNDS**, try blowing across the mouths of bottles filled to various levels with water so that a melody can be played on them. An **AMPHIGORY** is a nonsense rhyme, like the words to the song *Oh Suzannah*: "It rained all night the day I left,/ The weather it was dry;/ The sun so hot I froze to death,/ Suzannah, don't you cry!" Does anyone remember this old song?

© 2003 J&J Lundquist

# ambi

**[AHM bee]　on both sides, around, surround**

ambidextrous (dexter L. - right) – able to use both hands with equal skill (to have two right hands)
ambivalent (valens, valentis L. - strong, powerful) – to be attracted and repulsed at the same time; undecided
ambiguous (agere L. - to drive) – doubtful or uncertain; a feeling of being driven in two or more directions
ambience (ire L. - to go) – environment, surroundings, atmosphere
ambisinister (sinister L. - left) – to have two left hands; clumsy

**TEACHING NOTES:** These two words, **AMPHI** and **AMBI**, are good examples of the change from the Greek to the Roman alphabet. When the Romans adopted Greek words, the Greek letter ϕ (**phi**) usually became "f" at the beginning, and "b" in the middle of a Latin word. You will notice in the list of derivatives that the partner root words in compound English words are mostly Latin root words with **AMBI** and Greek root words with **AMPHI** (but not always!).

For you baseball fans out there, a switch-hitter is **AMBIDEXTROUS**, someone who bats equally well from both sides of home plate. It's an interesting experiment to have your students practice writing a sentence with their dominant hands and then with the opposite ones and compare the results. Someone could find out how many "lefties" there are in the class and whether there are any **AMBIDEXTROUS** students. Figure the percentages! Left-handed pitchers in baseball are much in demand.

Children may feel **AMBIVALENT** about the end of a school year. They may have mixed emotions, such as excitement about a vacation but sadness at the prospect of not seeing their friends. Many people enjoy the romantic **AMBIENCE** that candlelight brings to a dinner table.

The word **AMBISINISTER** is almost never used any more since it means clumsy or one who has "two left hands." Because the majority of people throughout history have been right-handed, they did not understand why some people were naturally left-handed. They thought there must be something wrong with left-handed people. However, most left-handed children are unusually bright and skillful and excel at many activities when adults do not try to force them to become right-handed. Try finding some famous left-handers on the Internet!

© 2003 J&J Lundquist

**GREEK**
εu

# eu

### [EH oo]  well, good, pleasant

**eulogy** (<u>logos</u> G. - word, Vol. I, p. 15) – a speech of praise for a deceased person

**euphony** (<u>phone</u> G. - sound, Vol. I, p. 11) – pleasing sounds of a voice or music

**euphoria** (<u>pherein</u> G. - to bear) – a feeling of well-being or elation

**evangelist** (<u>angelos</u> G. - messenger) – one who brings good news

**eugenics** (<u>eugenes</u> G. - wellborn) – relating to or fitted for the production of good offspring

**euphemism** (<u>pheme</u> G. - speech) – substitution of a mild or indirect word for one which is thought to be offensive or blunt

**TEACHING NOTES:** While many Greek or Latin prepositions stand alone as separate words (ad, ab, in, com - see Vol. I), **EU** seldom stood alone in Greek sentences but was almost always used as a prefix. To keep language fresh and interesting, it can be fun to find as many **EUPHEMISMS** as possible for certain less-favored expressions (e.g., "powder room" for *toilet*, or "passed on" for *died*). There is usually no need to explore dysphemisms (deliberately using a more unpleasant expression than necessary), as children will undoubtedly encounter many of these because of their "shock value" in slang. Creativity with language should be encouraged in a positive direction!

When the Greek word **euaggelistos**, meaning "bringer of good news," was absorbed into English, the "u" was changed to "v" for easier pronunciation. "Gg" is pronounced as though it were "ng," and so we have our word **EVANGELIST** usually referring to someone spreading the "good news" of Christianity.

Students may ask about the name of the continent of **EUROPE**. It has an obscure origin. Among the Greek myths is the story of **EUROPA**, the beautiful, well-favored daughter of the King of Phoenicia. Her name is reminiscent of the word **euroclydon**, meaning east wind (which blows toward the west). Zeus fell in love with her and, temporarily changing himself into a beautiful white bull, carried her over the sea from Phoenicia toward the west and installed her as Queen of Crete. After Zeus dropped his disguise, **EUROPA** bore him three sons. The long history of **EUROPEAN** civilization dates back to about 3000 B.C., when King Minos, son of **EUROPA**, developed the Minoan civilization on the island of Crete. Minoans had a written language, skilled craftsmen, architects, and painters. Their culture spread first to other islands in the Aegean Sea, then to mainland Greece, to the Middle East with Alexander the Great, to Italy with the Romans, and on up throughout the continent. Voila! **EUROPEAN** (Western) civilization!

© 2003 J&J Lundquist

LATIN

# malus

### [MAH loos]    bad, ugly, evil, ill

malady (malade *French* - sick) – illness, any undesirable condition
malediction (dicere L. - to speak, Vol. I, p. 94) – words spoken badly of someone
malefactor (facere L. - to do, make, Vol. I, p. 91) – to do evil or wrong
dismal (dies L. - day) – evil or unlucky; dreary, causing gloom
malaria (aer L. - air) – bad air; a disease carried by some mosquitos
malevolent (velle L. - to wish) – having evil wishes or intentions
malice – desire to cause pain, injury, or distress to another
malign – to utter injuriously misleading or false reports; to speak evil of
Malapropism – use of an inappropriate word in place of a correct one

**TEACHING NOTES:** At the time of the American Revolution, 1775, an English playwright, Richard Brinsley Sheridan, brought out a play called ***The Rivals***. The most memorable character in the play is **Mrs. Malaprop**, who was so named because she always used words inappropriately, usually to hilarious effect. Here are a few of her thoughts on education from Act I, Scene II:

*"Observe, Sir Anthony, I would not wish a child of mine to be a progeny (prodigy) of learning! ... She should have a supercilious (superficial) knowledge of accounts and be instructed in geometry (geography) that she might know something of the contagious (contiguous) countries; and she should be mistress of orthodoxy (orthography) that she might not misspell and mispronounce words so shamefully as girls usually do, and likewise that she might reprehend (comprehend) the true meaning of what she is saying."*

It's a bit of a task to sort out what she meant to say in place of what she actually said. However, theatergoers in the 18th century had such good working vocabularies that they could instantly catch her blunders, and Mrs. Malaprop usually had the whole theater rocking with laughter!

The sickness known as **MALARIA** was originally thought to be caused by bad air, but scientists discovered that it was spread by certain kinds of mosquitos. It has been wiped out in the United States. Other parts of the world are still working on its eradication.

The French have a large collection of words which begin with **MAL** - but, of course, French began as a Gallic dialect of Latin. The beautiful little chateau, where Josephine, the wife of Napoleon, lived after their divorce, is called **Malmaison**, which, ironically, means "sick or wretched house" because of the ravages the house suffered from invading Normans in the 9th century. Josephine's loving care restored the beauty of the chateau. She surrounded it with exquisite roses, one of which was named **Malmaison** to commemorate the chateau. This rose is known to gardeners all over the world.

© 2003 J&J Lundquist

# e-
# ex

**LATIN**

### [AY, EKS]   out of; beyond; from; former

exit (ire L. - to go) – to go out; the door through which you leave
exclude (claudere L. - to shut) – to shut out of a group
evidence (videre L. - to see, Vol. I, p. 14) – out of what can be seen
elaborate (laborare L. - to work) – to work out in great detail
effort (fortis L. - strong) – strenuous physical or mental exertion
elect (legere L. - to choose) – to pick out; vote for
educate (ducere L. - to lead) – to lead out of ignorance
excel (excellere L. - to rise or project) – to rise above expectations
except (capere L. - to take) – taken away from a general rule
erase (radere L. - to scrape) – to rub out or obliterate
eruption (rumpere L. - to break) – to break out or burst open
evacuate (vacuare L. - to make empty) – to empty out; to withdraw

**TEACHING NOTES:** Every family and school should know how to **EXIT** a building in case of a fire or other disaster. Perhaps students could help their families be prepared by drawing a map of potential **EXIT** routes and discussing what to do in case of an emergency.

To **EXCLUDE** some from a group is to separate them out, usually because of different characteristics. Everyone should **EXCLUDE** swear words from his or her vocabulary. **EVIDENCE** is information or an object that helps you find the truth by examining what you can see. Woodcarving can either be simple or **ELABORATE** ("e-LÁ-bor-it"), the latter showing that great care and **EFFORT** were put into creating details. If someone gives a one-word answer to a question, one might ask him to "e-LA-bor-ATE," or to explain in detail how he got his answer.

Americans **ELECT** a president every four years. Students might like to research what requirements there are to becoming an eligible candidate for president, or for any office. Parents and teachers **EDUCATE** children to help them grow up to be responsible citizens. Mt. St. Helens, in Washington state, **ERUPTED** in 1980. Seismologists had detected earthquakes and a rise in temperature below the layers of rock in the mountain, and many people decided to **EVACUATE** the area.

**EXTRA WORDS:** **EVICT** (vincere L. - to conquer) – to legally force a tenant out of a building.
**EXPATRIATE** (patria L. - fatherland) – one exiled from or living outside his native country.

© 2003 J&J Lundquist

# archos

**GREEK**

αρχος

**[AHR koss]    chief, principal, primative**

archaeology (<u>logos</u> G. - study, Vol. I, p. 15) – study of the beginnings of man

archaic – very old; from the earliest times

archbishop (<u>episkopos</u> G. - overseer) – leader of bishops

archduke (<u>dux</u> L. - leader) – first in rank among other dukes

architect (<u>techton</u> G. - craftsman) – one who designs new buildings

hierarchy (<u>heiros</u> G. - holy, sacred) – any system of persons ranked one above the other

monarchy (<u>monos</u> G. - alone) – rule by one person

oligarchy (<u>oligos</u> G. - few) – rule by a few persons

patriarch (<u>pater</u> L. - father, Vol. I, p. 78) – founding father of a family or country; ruling father figure

**TEACHING NOTES:** Do you wonder why we didn't include **ARCH** in the derivatives above? Well, **ARCH** is from the **Latin** word **ARCUS**, and while there are **ARCHES** in churches where **ARCHBISHOPS** oversee the church organization, they don't necessarily oversee the **ARCHES**! (See the next page for **ARCUS**.) Actually, an **ARCHBISHOP** is a leader, a ruler, a step higher in church **HIERARCHY** from the bishop level. He oversees the bishops, who, in turn, oversee the priests and nuns and other church workers. The word "bishop" is from two Greek words, **EPI**, a preposition meaning "on, upon, over" and **SKOPEO** (Vol. I, p. 13) meaning "see." The Greeks combined these for their word **EPISKOPOS** - overseer, from which the Episcopal Church derives its name. (It is governed by bishops rather than by a pope and cardinals.) **HIERARCHY** means organization into orders or ranks, each subordinate to the one above. In fact, when Henry VIII, England's **MONARCH**, who was Catholic, asked the Pope for a divorce and wasn't granted one, he founded the Church of England, so that he wouldn't be subordinate to anyone in the church **HIERARCHY**. This episode in English history makes for quite an interesting research project!

An **ARCHITECT** may use arches in his buildings, or he may not. Historically, the **ARCHI-** part of his title means he is the top person on a building project, the designer, the leader, the master builder. The skill of **ARCHITECTS** has been developing for thousands of years. The ancient Egyptians understood the scientific principle behind arches and perhaps one of their **ARCHITECTS** designed the first arch, but it was the Etruscan and Roman **ARCHITECTS** who used **ARCHES** extensively. They enabled the Romans to build larger and more impressive buildings, such as the Colosseum, where many people could gather for entertainment.

© 2003 J&J Lundquist

# arcus

**LATIN**

### [AHR koos]   bow, arc

arc – part of a circle
arch – curved structure built to support weight over an opening
arcade – a row of arches supported by pillars
archer – one who shoots arrows with a bow; the constellation Sagittarius
archery – the sport of shooting arrows from a bow
archway – an entrance or passage under an arch
overarching – spanning as with an arch; over everything below

**TEACHING NOTES:** The Egyptians knew something about **ARCHES**. The Greeks preferred to build temples using upright columns, bridging the distance between them with long flat stones. While the Greeks did not invent this concept, the style is associated with them because the Parthenon, in Athens, illustrates this beautiful Greek contribution to architecture. The primitive construction of Stonehenge in England also shows this "post and lintel" style of building. The Romans, wanting to build on yet a grander scale, used the **ARCH** to span ever wider spaces. Long, strong lintel stones are hard to find and to transport. However, **ARCHES** can be built using a series of smaller, cleverly shaped stones, which can span a wide space beneath them and support much heavier weight above that space. The Romans used this structure to build bridges, temples, triumphal **ARCHES**, and long **ARCADES** to use as aqueducts and to construct buildings several stories high—such as the Colosseum in Rome.

Figuring out how to shape stones so that they could bridge a distance longer than a single long lintel stone could reach was the work of some very brilliant minds! A Web site at *www.sciencefirst.com* gives you instruction in how to build a Roman arch with your students. They will sell you a beautiful little model of fine hardwood pieces that will last for years of classes so you and your students can construct an **ARCH** time and again to observe the architectural principles at work.

Children can learn the parts of a simple **ARCH**: the wedge-shaped *arch stones*, rising from *springers* up to the *keystone*; the *crown* (highest part underneath the arch); the *haunches*; the *span* and the *buttresses*. Discuss the necessity for buttresses (or even flying buttresses) to counter the outward thrust of the **ARCH** stones (Notre Dame in Paris is a prime example of this). Sometimes **ARCHES** stand next to other **ARCHES**, in an **ARCADE**, or across a river, stream, or other space to be bridged. Every school library should have a copy of David Macauley's beautifully illustrated book *Cathedral* in which the use of **ARCHES** in Medieval churches is explained in detail. It will provide hours of enjoyment for students who want to know more about **ARCHES**.

© 2003 J&J Lundquist

LATIN

# circum

### [KEER coom]   around, about

circle – a perfectly round plane figure
circumference (ferre L. - to bear) – the line that forms a circle
circus – a round arena surrounded by seating for performances by trained animals, acrobats, clowns, etc.
circa – around or about, used with dates which are not exact
circuit (ire L. - to go) – to go or travel around; a circular journey
circulation – movement in a circular motion or course
circumscribe (scribere L. - write) – to draw a boundary line around
circumstance (stare L. - to stand) – that which stands around or surrounds; conditions existing at a certain time
circumspect (spectare L. - look carefully; watch) – look all around

**TEACHING NOTES:** The ancient Romans held horse and chariot races in an elongated oval surrounded by seats, which was called a **CIRCUS**. The **Circus Maximus** in Rome was the largest of these arenas. Perhaps students have seen the one depicted in the movie ***Ben Hur***. Our modern **CIRCUSES**, with or without animals, are exhibitions named for the **CIRCULAR** rings in which they usually take place.

Historians often use **CIRCA** to indicate their best guess as to when an event may have occurred. They use a small *c* followed by a period in front of a date to indicate an approximation. For example, "c. 1400" would indicate that something took place in or around the year 1400.

In homes everywhere, electricity travels along wires (usually copper) from its source (the power wires outside the house) to a **CIRCUIT** breaker or fuse box, and from there through **CIRCUITS** (long loops of insulated wire) to various electrically driven lights or appliances. Each **CIRCUIT** is designed to supply a specific amount of electrical power and no more. If you ask a **CIRCUIT** to supply more power than it is designed to carry—if you plug too many appliances into a **CIRCUIT**—it will trip the breaker or blow the fuse. The power company measures how much electricity you use and sends you a bill.

Money as it is passed around from person to person is said to be in **CIRCULATION**. When discussing the **CIRCULATION** of a newspaper or magazine, you are describing how many readers the publication has. The **CIRCULATION** of the blood is from the heart to the arteries and back through the veins to the heart. One who is **CIRCUMSPECT** is cautious and looks around to be aware of the **CIRCUMSTANCES** around him, paying attention to anything that might affect decisions or actions.

**Extra Words:** A **CIRCUITOUS** (sir-*cue*-it-us) route is a roundabout or indirect path.

© 2003 J&J Lundquist

GREEK

κυκλος

# kyklos

**[KOOK loss, KIK loss]    ring, circle, wheel**

cycle – any complete round or recurring series
bicycle (bi G. - two) – rider-propelled vehicle with two wheels
tricycle (tri G. - three) – rider-propelled vehicle with three wheels
motorcycle – two- or three-wheeled vehicle propelled by a motor
cyclometer (metron G. - measure, Vol. I, p. 4) – an instrument for
        measuring arcs; device for recording the revolutions of a wheel
cyclone – a storm characterized by circular wind motion; a tornado
encyclopedia (paideia G. - child rearing, education) – a series of
        books of knowledge needed for a well-rounded education
Cyclops (ops G. - eye) – any of a group of giants in Greek mythology
        having a single round eye in the middle of the forehead

**TEACHING NOTES:** The ancient word **KYKLOS** has long been used to describe **CYCLICAL** (circular) patterns of the natural world, such as the rising and setting of the sun and the moon and the coming and going of the seasons of the year. Observing additional familiar **CYCLES** of life (birth to death) led man to realize he could learn from and build on what others had done before to improve and lengthen life on earth. Think together about changes in the history and situation of man from the earliest times. What inventions have increased the length or quality of human life? Where are we in a **CYCLE** today?

The **CYCLOPES** in Greek myths were the unfortunate sons of Gaea, Mother Earth, and Uranus, the Sky. The **CYCLOPES** shared the distinguishing feature of one grotesque eye in the middle of their foreheads. These huge unsightly beings were the smiths and masons to the gods, building the palace of the gods at the summit of Mt. Olympus and fashioning thunderbolts for Zeus.

If a person begins to read a good **ENCYCLOPEDIA** from beginning to end, he will have a vast and comprehensive education. However, **ENCYCLOPEDIAS** usually serve as a storehouse of knowledge for a person to consult when he needs information about a particular subject. It would be wonderful if every classroom and family could have a good **ENCYCLOPEDIA** on hand to support lifelong education.

Older students might be interested in researching "**CYCLICAL** stocks." These are stocks in companies producing products for which demand fluctuates with the rise and fall of the economy: automobiles, heavy appliances, production machinery, raw metals, et al.

© 2003 J&J Lundquist

**GREEK**

περι

# peri

> **[PEH ree]    around**
>
> **perimeter** (<u>metron</u> G. - measure, Vol. I, p. 4) – distance around outside of an area
>
> **periscope** (<u>skopein</u> G. - to look, Vol. I, p. 13) – device for seeing around obstacles
>
> **perigee** (<u>geo</u> G. - earth, Vol. I, p. 56) – that point in the moon's orbit closest to earth
>
> **perihelion** (<u>helios</u> G. - sun, Vol. I, p. 51) – that point in the orbit of a planet, comet, or other heavenly body that is nearest to the sun
>
> **period** (<u>odos</u> G. - way, path) – completion of a cycle; dot at end of a sentence
>
> **peripatetic** (<u>patein</u> G. - to tread) – walking about, itinerant
>
> **peripheral** (<u>pherein</u> G. - to carry) – carry around the outside; extra
>
> **peristyle** (<u>stylos</u> G. - pillar) – colonnade surrounding a building or courtyard

**TEACHING NOTES:** Surely among the greatest contributions of the Greeks to civilization was Euclidian geometry, the branch of mathematics taught by Euclid for measuring the circumference of the earth and the area of various parts of it. Geometry enables you to calculate spaces within the **PERIMETERS** of soccer and football fields, classrooms, homes, and other areas.

In a submarine, a **PERISCOPE** allows you to look above the surface of the water while the boat is still under water. It is fun to make a **PERISCOPE** with milk cartons and pocket mirrors so short people can see over tall people at a parade or other gathering.

To really understand **PERIGEE** and **PERIHELION**, teachers need to talk with students about the orbiting paths of planets, satellites, comets, and other heavenly bodies as these objects travel around the earth or the sun. Orbits aren't perfectly round, but rather follow an elliptical, or egg-shaped course. The earth or the sun isn't at the exact center of the ellipse, so the planet or comet travels closer to the earth or sun on part of its elliptical journey, (**PERIGEE** or **PERIHELION**) and further away at the other end of the ellipse (**APOGEE** or **APHELION**, from **apo** G. – away from). Students can find wonderful pictures of the movements of the Solar System in the library or on the Internet, which make this very clear.

We call the dot at the end of a sentence a **PERIOD**. It shows that we have followed the path of a single thought, and having come to the end, we make a full stop.

Aristotle, the Greek philosopher, was a **PERIPATETIC** teacher because he walked around Athens, and in a **PERISTYLE** called the Stoa, asking questions for his students to think about and answer.

© 2003 J&J Lundquist

GREEK

θεος

# theos

### [TAY oss]  god

**theology** (<u>logos</u> G. - word, study, Vol. I, p. 15) — knowledge or study of god
**monotheism** (<u>monos</u> G. - alone, solitary) — belief in one god
**polytheism** (<u>poly</u> G. - many) — belief in many gods
**atheist** (<u>a</u>, <u>ab</u> L. - away from) — one who does not believe in any god
**theocracy** (<u>kratos</u> G. - power) — government of a state by rulers seen as divinely guided in accordance with laws of one religion
**Pantheon** (<u>pan</u> G. - all) — temple in Rome built to worship all the Roman gods
**enthusiasm** (<u>in</u> L. - in, into) — having spirit or a god inside; inspiration
**Dorothy** (<u>doron</u> G. - gift) — girl's name meaning gift of god
**Theodore** (<u>doron</u> G. - gift) — boy's name meaning gift of god

**TEACHING NOTES:** Since the Romans were **POLYTHEISTIC** (believing in many gods), they were afraid of making any one god jealous by building a temple to another. Their solution to this dilemma was to build the **PANTHEON**, a temple to all the gods, so that none would feel slighted. The Romans wanted to create a large open space inside the temple so that many citizens could worship at the same time. They invented concrete as a building material, and the strength of the concrete enabled them to create a large dome. The dome had a hole in the top so the worshippers could look up to the sky where the gods lived. The **PANTHEON** in Rome was the first domed building ever built. Since then, builders have used the concept of the dome on many important buildings around the world, including Hagia Sofia in Istanbul, St. Peter's Church in Rome, and the U. S. Capitol Building in Washington, D. C. Perhaps a clever student investigator could find a picture of the Pantheon in the library. Then, a sleuth might read the carved inscription over the front entrance and tell the class which Roman emperor had it built, and when! (Use the page on Roman numerals – Appendix I.)

The concept of **THEOCRACY** is worth thinking about. Nations in which there is a dominant religion and in which religious rulers have authority *in both civil and religious matters* may be called **THEOCRACIES**. Can a country in which most citizens believe in a god but adhere to churches of many different denominations be called a **THEOCRACY**?

Parents who name a child **DOROTHY, DOROTHEA, THEODORA,** or **THEODORE, THEODORIC,** or **THEODOSIUS** have found a nice way of expressing their happiness with the new family member.

© 2003 J&J Lundquist

# deus

**[day oos]　god**

deity – having the character of a god, object of worship; a god
deify – to exalt to the position of a god; to treat as a god
deist – one who believes in God but rejects the organized religions
adieu (a L. - to + dieu *French* - god) – parting salutation, go with God
addio (ad L. - to + dio *Italian* - god) – Goodbye, Farewell
adios (a L. to + dios *Spanish* - god) – parting wish; Goodbye
deus ex machina – "day oos eks ma kee na" – god from machine

**TEACHING NOTES:** It's fascinating to see how interrelated are the words for "day" (**dies**) and god, goddess (**deus, dea, divum, diva**). Back in the old Indo-European vocabulary, di, diu, dyu, dju, div all had meanings like "bright, shining, gleaming," etc. Since many of the prehistoric people worshiped the sun, it was a natural progression for these old word parts to become the raw materials out of which to make such Latin words for their gods as **deus**, a noun, and **divinus**, the related adjective (see p. 24). **Zeus, Jove, Diana**, all names for classical deities, were various pronunciations of these early words meaning god and god-like.

The Romans used i, instead of j, as in Iulius Caesar. The J was invented later by printers to prevent confusion in reading words beginning with iu such as **ius** (law), **iungo** (join), etc.

In plays in ancient Greek theatres, sometimes the story progressed until the plot seemed impossible to untangle, whereupon an actor portraying a god descended from above to the stage by means of a sort of crane or system of pulleys and resolved the conflict by divine decree. In the modern theatre, such devices are sometimes used (e.g., a poor, struggling, young couple tries for two and a half acts to avoid foreclosure on their mortgage, only to be saved just before the final curtain by the news of a legacy from a rich uncle). This is still described as **DEUS EX MACHINA**, but is not considered good playwriting.

The Romance languages—French, Italian, Portuguese, Romanian, and Spanish—evolved from Latin since those countries were part of the Roman Empire. They all have words used when friends mean to lovingly commend the other to the care of God. The French say "**ADIEU**;" the Spanish, "**ADIOS**" or "**VAYA CON DIOS**" (go with God); and the Italians, "**ADDIO**."

LATIN

© 2003 J&J Lundquist

LATIN

# divinus

**[dee WEE noos]     god-like**

divine (adjective) – relating to or proceeding directly from God or a god

divine (noun) – a soothsayer, a clergyman, a theologian

divine (verb) – to discover as if led by God; find water with divining rod

diviner – one who can predict or foretell events, a prophet or soothsayer

divine right of kings – the right to rule comes from God and not the people

diva – a goddess; a celebrated woman opera singer

**TEACHING NOTES:** Throughout history, when men performed mystifying acts like finding water or minerals underground with a stick they called a **DIVINING ROD**, they claimed a direct connection with the supernatural and called themselves **DIVINERS**. In Shakespeare's play, ***Julius Caesar***, it was a **DIVINER** or soothsayer (whom some might call a psychic today) who warned Caesar to "Beware the Ides of March." This was a foretelling of the ambush that Caesar would face from his friend Brutus and some jealous senators when he arrived at the Senate that day.

France's "Sun King," Louis XIV, believed in the **DIVINE RIGHT OF KINGS**, which meant that he inherited the right to be king from God and that none of his subjects should question that right. It was this belief that led Louis to spend enormous amounts of money from France's treasury to build his palace at Versailles, while many of the French people went hungry. Louis' successors, Louis XV and Louis XVI, inherited his attitude and his debts. Though France, under Louis XVI, came to the aid of American colonists in their struggle for independence from Britain, the ideas on which the American Revolution was based (that *all* men are created equal and that government can receive power only *from the people* it governs) could not help but influence the French people. Fed up with crippling taxes and royalty that ignored their plight, the French people started their own revolution in 1789.

The greatest female opera singers throughout history have been referred to as **DIVAS**, perhaps to acknowledge their talent as a gift from God. In recent years, the term **DIVA** has been more loosely applied to pop stars. The term has taken on the connotation of describing people with large egos, who are difficult to work with. In the 18th and 19th centuries, opera stars were the pop stars of their day. Students who have never heard a good recording of a famous aria sung by Maria Callas, Leontyne Price, Beverly Sills, or Kiri Te Kanawa (to name just a few) may be amazed at the range of emotion the human voice can convey. Arias or duets by Puccini, Bizet, or Mozart are good introductions to the world of opera, and may awaken a student's interest in a world of passion and drama beyond the realm of modern popular music and music videos.

© 2003 J&J Lundquist

# homo hominis

**[HOH mo, HOH mi nis]   man, human being**

homo sapiens (sapire L. - to be wise) – man as a thinking species
homage – oath of loyalty by a vassal or tenant to a feudal lord
human – relating to or characteristic of human beings
humane – marked by compassion for humans or animals
homunculus – a little man, a dwarf
ad hominem – attacks against a man personally rather than at his ideas or policies

**TEACHING NOTES:** HOMO SAPIENS is the name given to early man as he became distinct from other early upright, two-legged species such as **HOMO ERECTUS** who walked on two legs. **HOMO SAPIENS NEANDERTHALENSIS**, a "thinking cave man," lived more than 35,000 years ago. His skeleton was found in the Neanderthal Valley in western Germany. Scientists considered him to be a **HUMAN** of considerable intelligence. Even smarter was **HOMO SAPIENS SAPIENS**, the name given to Cro-Magnon man, who had many of the characteristics of modern man. A series of books written by Jean Auel, beginning with *The Clan of the Cave Bear*, presents a vivid picture of life for these two groups of ancient human beings.

In feudal times in Europe, when powerful nobles owned most of the land and people who worked the land were serfs or vassals, the vassal swore **HOMAGE**, or pledged his loyalty to and dependence on the feudal lord, saying, in effect, "I'm your man."

The Romance languages have words for **man** which are very close to Latin: **HOMBRE** (*Spanish*); **HOMME** (*French*); and **UOMO** (*Italian*).

We use the Latin phrase **AD HOMINEM** to describe the debating technique which attacks an opponent personally rather than produces arguments against his ideas or policies. Teachers should encourage students to examine the newspapers at election time to try to discern which candidates are arguing honestly for or against ideas and which are simply making **AD HOMINEM** attacks.

**HOMUNCULUS** is an example of a Latin diminutive form meaning a small or tiny version of the basic noun, **HOMO**. A tiny man could be a dwarf, elf, or leprechaun. Another diminutive, **musculus**, meaning a small mouse, is the root word behind our English word "**muscle**," named, no doubt, in earlier, less scientific times, for the illusion that when one is flexing his biceps, quads, or abs, small mice are playing under the skin. We aren't kidding. Look it up!

© 2003 J&J Lundquist

GREEK

ανθροπος

# anthropos

**[AHN troh poss]   man, mankind, humankind**

**anthropology** (logos G. - word, study, Vol. I, p. 15) – the study of mankind
**anthropomorphic** (morph G. - form, shape) – having human form
**anthropomorphize** – attribute humanity to animals or things
**philanthropy** (philein G. - to love, Vol. I, p. 6) – devotion to human welfare
**philanthropist** – a generous giver to education, charity, or social work
**misanthrope** (misein G. - to hate) – a hater or distruster of mankind

**TEACHING NOTES:** The Greeks used the word *ANTHROPOS* to mean **man** as opposed to *beasts*, whereas they used the word *ANDROS* when referring to **man** as opposed to *woman*. There are fewer derivatives for **ANDROS** in English than there are for **ANTHROPOS**. However, the derivative word **ANDROID,** meaning a robot or mechanical creature in the shape of a man, is widely known (think of *Data* in *Star Trek–The Next Generation* or *C3PO* in *Star Wars*).

Don't confuse the "mis-" in **MISANTHROPE,** which comes from the Greek word meaning "to hate," with the old Anglo-Saxon prefix "mis-" meaning "wrong or bad." To misdirect someone means to make a mistake in directions, but there is not necessarily any hatred involved. A miscarriage of justice, on the other hand, may involve misdeeds (crimes) or a miscreant (a criminal or villain), suggesting a close relationship between the two ideas of hate and error. Intent is usually an indication of "will to," and courts seek to determine motivation, and what is meant by a "mistake."

The great French dramatist, Moliere, wrote a play called *The Misanthrope,* in which the main character finds all mankind inferior to himself.

Our country has been blessed by many **PHILANTHROPISTS** who have provided museums, libraries, universities, and foundations of all kinds. Can the class think of people who have given generously for the benefit of their fellow citizens? Students might create a bulletin board about them.

Mickey and Minnie Mouse, and Stuart Little are examples of **ANTHROPOMORPHIZED** mice. Students may have favorite stories in which animals have been **ANTHROPOMORPHIZED**, in which animal characters speak to each other or to humans and exhibit thoughts and feelings that humans would have under similar circumstances. *Charlotte's Web*, by E. B. White, or the movie *Babe* have lots of **ANTHROPOMORPHIZED** characters with whom students may already be acquainted.

© 2003 J&J Lundquist

LATIN

# vir

**[WEER]   man, manly, masculine**

virile – manly
virago – a man-like woman
triumvirate (tri L. - three) – a three-man governing team
virtue – manly strength or courage; moral excellence
virtual – being in essence or effect, but not in fact
virtuoso – a man with great technical skill in the fine arts, esp. music

**TEACHING NOTES:** The word **VIR** means **man** as opposed to woman. Therefore, **VIRILE** qualities are those which are distinctly male. A man's **VIRILITY** or manliness is exemplified by the qualities he exhibits, such as strength, courage, and morality.

A **VIRAGO** is a woman who has man-like qualities. She is tough, tall, or strong, or one who simply lacks those gentle, feminine qualities which the world admires and needs.

A **TRIUMVIRATE** is a three-man team, which divides the responsibilites of a head of state among themselves. The most famous **TRIUMVIRATE** in Rome was the team of Caesar, Pompey, and Crassus.

The ancient Romans had developed ideas about the qualities they thought the ideal man, **VIR**, should have. In more recent centuries, as they built the British Empire, the English tried to use many of the best features of the Roman Empire—the "Pax Romana" (Roman Peace) as it was called. The knights of King Arthur's Round Table had their origin here. Many people believe that Arthur (Arturus) was a Roman general. As the English extended British influence around the world, the qualities of character which the British admired in the noblest Romans were ones they tried to cultivate in themselves. Rudyard Kipling, who lived in India during the time of the British colonial rule, wrote a poem, *If*. It tells you how to go about becoming that ideal man whom the Romans called **VIR**.

We hope students will study, in connection with this word, **VIR**, Rudyard Kipling's poem, *If*; you can find it on the Internet. Any school student who can recite from memory all 32 lines of the poem will receive a keepsake award. To the publisher's address below, please send a letter which includes a teacher's note verifying that accomplishment:

LITERACY UNLIMITED, P.O. Box 278, Medina, WA 98039.

© 2003 J&J Lundquist

# femina

**[FAY mi nah]   woman**

female – the gender that can produce eggs or bear offspring
feminine – having qualities associated with women
femininity – state of being womanly
effeminate – feminine in appearance or manner; unmasculine
feminism – advocacy of women's rights
*femme fatale* (*French*) – an irresistibly attractive woman

**TEACHING NOTES:** The Romans had another word **mulier mulieris** for woman which the Latin dictionary tells us is related to **mollis**—from which we get **mollify**, meaning to placate, soften, calm down—and to **mollusk**, which are those soft-bodied creatures such as snails, mussels, clams, oysters, and (oh dear!) slugs. There are very few English derivatives from **mulier** (**muliebrity**, one meaning being "femininity"—found in the dictionary between **mule** and **mulish**) which the feminine half of the English-speaking world would appreciate having applied to them. Roman men apparently meant for it to refer to that agreeable, pliant, ego-enhancing, hard working, uncomplaining little woman whom they liked to anticipate coming home to.

A thousand years later, when Latin began to pervade English after the Norman invasion of 1066, those good Anglo-Saxon women would have none of it, and **FEMINA**, and its derivatives, had to suffice to describe the biological functions, the physical weaknesses, and the spiritual strengths of women. The word **woman**, which we use all the time, was originally "wif - mann" or wife of a man. The Latin word **VIRGO** referred to a young unmarried woman, whereas **VIRGA** meant a green twig, or a green slip for planting, and also a magic wand. By such interesting mental associations has vocabulary developed and evolved.

On a more elevated note, a **FEMININE** version of Rudyard Kipling's poem *If*, written by Elizabeth Lincoln Otis entitled *An IF for Girls*, describing ideal womanhood, can be found with a search of the Internet. The student who can recite it from memory and sends a letter to the publisher, including a note from a teacher verifying that accomplishment, will receive a keepsake award.
LITERACY UNLIMITED, P.O. Box 278, Medina, WA 98039.

© 2003 J&J Lundquist

# infans
# infantis

**[EEN fans, een FAHN tis]   inability to speak**

infant – speechless; one who cannot yet speak
infancy – condition of being an infant; early childhood
infantile – behaving like an infant or child
Infanta (*Spanish*) – daughter of the King and Queen of Spain or Portugal who is not heir to the throne
Infante (*Spanish*) – son of the King and Queen of Sprain or Portugal who is not heir to the throne
infant school (in Britain) – school for children under seven years old
infantry – (originally) force composed of those too young or inexperienced or low in rank for cavalry service; (now) foot soldiers in an army
infanticipate – to be in a state of expecting the birth of a child

**TEACHING NOTES:** It's interesting to realize that the original meaning of **INFANT** is "one who cannot yet speak." So, learning to speak, to use one's native language, is a large and important part of growing up. Conversing with children, reading stories to them, listening to their ideas, comments, and observations—all language activities—are as vital as food and exercise in the development of the small human beings in our care. A delay or omission of this vital verbal nourishment may result in reticence or the inability of the child to speak clearly and confidently, and may cause him or her to remain **INFANTILE** indefinitely.

In both Spain and Portugal the **INFANTE** is a son and the **INFANTA**, a daughter, of the king and queen, but neither is a first heir to the throne. The first heir is called the Principe. In England, the title of this position is "the Crown Prince."

It is difficult to imagine that our present-day **INFANTRY**, the backbone of the military forces which protect the entire country, was so named in the 16th century because **INFANTRY** forces consisted of very young foot soldiers too inexperienced with horses to join the cavalry!

© 2003 J&J Lundquist

GREEK

παις

# pais paidos

### [pah EES, peye DOSS]  child

**pediatrician** (<u>iatros</u> G. - physician) – a doctor for children

**encyclopedia** (<u>kyklos</u> G. - round) – a series of books which provide a child a well-rounded knowledge on all subjects

**pedagogue** (<u>agein</u> G. - to lead) – tutor who escorted children to school

**pedagogy** – art or skill of teaching children

**paideia** – education of children in all aspects of their society

**pedant** – person who makes an excessive or inappropriate display of learning

**pedantic** – overly concerned with minute details and formalities in teaching

**pedantry** – slavish attention to formal rules or minute details

**TEACHING NOTES:** Words like **PEDIATRICIAN**, **PEDAGOGUE**, and **ENCYCLOPEDIA**—from **PAIS, PAIDOS**—all have to do with children and their education.

The Greeks were pioneers in developing the whole field of education. There were those (especially in Sparta) who thought physical education and training should be most important, while others championed development of the intellect and morality. Others aimed at a balance. The great philosophers established schools. Plato founded the Academy. Aristotle taught rhetoric at the Academy, became the tutor of Alexander the Great, and founded the research institute called the Lyceum.

**PEDANT** (teacher), **PEDANTIC**, and **PEDANTRY** are derivatives from the same Greek root word for child. However, they refer to a kind of teacher (or learner) who stamps out the pleasure and excitement of learning for others. A **PEDANT** likes to show off his learning in boring detail. His teaching has nothing to do with children and everything to do with plodding self-glorification. Be gone, dull **PEDANTRY**!!!

**PAIDEIA** (pye-dee-uh) is a Greek word that has entered the English language unchanged. It means the whole education and upbringing of children. Some scholarly leaders, Mortimer Adler and Jaques Barzun among them, built a comprehensive curriculum for the education of children through high school. It is called *The Paideia Program*. In 1984, they published their syllabus, still available at the large Internet booksellers. Available, also, is E. D. Hirsch's excellent series of books on cultural literacy for grades K–6, called *What Your Kindergartener* (or *1st*, *2nd*, etc., *Grader*) *Needs to Know*.

© 2003 J&J Lundquist

GREEK

σχολε

# schole

### [SKOH lay]   leisure, free time

school – (n.) a place of education; a group of fish swimming together; (v.) to teach or educate

scholastic – of or pertaining to schools or school education

scholar – a student who is taught, especially one who is learned in classical (Greek and Latin) languages and literature

scholarly – pertaining to, or characterizing a scholar; learned, erudite

scholarship – the attainments of a scholar in learning; a grant-in-aid to a student at a school or university

**TEACHING NOTES:** How far we have moved from the original meaning of this Greek root word, **schole** (leisure), which gave us the derivatives **SCHOOL** and **SCHOLAR**! The modern requirement of compulsory **SCHOOLING** or education has altered the concept of learning as a privilege—as what one does with free time when working for a paycheck allows enough leisure to explore subjects in which one is interested. Now **SCHOOLING** has become something one is legally forced to do all through childhood. Unless children are made aware of the critical role they play in a free society, they can view school as drudgery and irrelevant to their daily lives. Thomas Jefferson understood that an educated public was the *sine qua non* (without which not) of the new American democracy, which he had helped create:

*"If a nation expects to be ignorant and free, in a state of civilization, it expects what never was and never will be.... If we are to guard against ignorance and remain free, it is the responsibility of every American to be informed."*

Thomas Jefferson in a letter to Col. Charles Yancey, January 6, 1816

The desire and determination to understand and function effectively in the world arrives as standard equipment in each baby that is born. Children are natural self-educators and the most valuable lessons we can teach them are how to use the tools by which they can continue to teach themselves all their lives. Learning the code of the English language is basic to exploring the written wisdom of the ages. An acquaintance with classical languages, from which much of our vocabulary has evolved, leads to deeper understanding of all printed material, ancient and contemporary. Facility with the use of libraries and the vast research resources of the Internet encourage independent **SCHOLARSHIP**. Another well-known quotation is:

*"Wisdom is the principal thing; therefore get wisdom; and with all thy getting, get understanding."*

(Proverbs 4:7)

© 2003 J&J Lundquist

LATIN

# ludo
# lusus

**[LOO do, LOO soos]   play, mock**

allude (<u>ad</u> L. - to, toward) – make indirect reference to; refer to
elude, elusive (<u>e</u>, <u>ex</u> L. - out of) – to avoid cleverly; to escape
delude (v.) (<u>de</u> L. - down, away from) – to play falsely, deceive
collude (v.) (<u>con</u> L. - with, together) – to conspire or plot
illusion (n.) (<u>in</u> L. - not) – the creation of a false impression of reality
illusory (adj.) – misleading, unreal
ludicrous – laughable, ridiculous, absurd
interlude (<u>interlude</u> L. - between) – music between parts of a longer performance
prelude (<u>prae</u> L. - before) – music played before the main performance
postlude (<u>post</u> L. - after) – music played after the main performance

**TEACHING NOTES:** The idea of "play" to speakers of Latin included amusement, imitation, and deception, as well as play acting, dance, sport, games of all kinds, education for young children, and training for gladiators! When we **ALLUDE** to something or someone, we suggest something that will bring to mind what we are talking about without actually saying it directly. "The man in the Oval Office" **ALLUDES** to the President of the United States. A fish that nibbles but never bites **ELUDES** the hook. If you can't remember a word, but it's "on the tip of your tongue," the word is **ELUSIVE**.

Unscrupulous advertisers may try to **DELUDE** you into buying products that will not do what they claim. Sometimes their claims are **LUDICROUS** and easily identifiable as dishonest. A person who aspires to an unrealistic goal is sometimes said to have "**DELUSIONS OF GRANDEUR**." Two pranksters may **COLLUDE** in playing a joke on someone. Two companies may agree to cooperate and charge higher prices rather than to compete fairly to see who can charge the lowest price. This is called **COLLUSION,** and it is illegal. A magician creates **ILLUSIONS** that seem like reality to his audience. When we attend church, a wedding, or any event, music that is playing as people gather is called a **PRELUDE**. Music played to usher people out is called a **POSTLUDE**. The music played during the "seventh-inning stretch" of a baseball game might be called an **INTERLUDE**.

© 2003 J&J Lundquist

GREEK

ιατρος

# iatros

**[yah TROSS]   doctor, physician, comforter**
psychiatrist (psychos G. - soul) – doctor for the mind and soul
podiatrist (podes G. - foot) – foot doctor
hippiatrist (hippos G. - horse) – a doctor for horses; a veterinarian
iatrology (logos G. - word, study) – the science of healing, a study of medical arts
pediatrician (paidos G. - child) – a children's physician
iatrogenic (genesis G. - origin, source) – illness or injury caused by doctors' mistakes
geriatrics (geron G. - old age) – field of medicine dealing with older people

**TEACHING NOTES:** In Greece of the 5th century B.C., people with ailments went to the Temple of Asclepius, the God of Healing (called Aesculapius by the Romans) for "incubation"; that is, they offered sacrifices and slept overnight in the temple hoping the god would reveal in a dream what should be done for a cure. Even the great philosopher, Socrates, as he was dying, said to his friend, Crito, *"I owe a rooster to Asclepius. Will you see that the debt is paid?"* An **IATROS** was a healer, or comforting caregiver to the sick and suffering, but was not much like our modern doctors of medical science.

The most famous doctor in ancient Greece was Hippocrates, who tried to find ways to cure sickness without depending on the unreliable moods of Asclepius and the dreams he might send to the sleeping temple "incubators." His followers had to abide by the Hippocratic Oath, *"First, do no harm,"* in their attempts to help people find cures for injuries, diseases, or suffering. For centuries these **iatri** (plural form) were mainly servants or even slaves. In Roman times, successful healers began to teach others in schools, and the status of doctors began to rise. In Christian times, charitable people founded hospitals for the care of the sick.

**IATROS** is used primarily as a prefix or suffix in English words that describe specialized fields of medicine. A **PSYCHIATRIST** is one who tries to find cures for disorders of the mind or soul. A **PODIATRIST** takes care of people's feet. A **HIPPIATRIST** is a veterinarian who specializes in taking care of horses. A **PEDIATRICIAN** specializes in keeping children healthy, and a doctor who tries to help old people practices **GERIATRICS**. Today, most doctors take the Hippocratic Oath and must swear to *"First, do no harm."* However, sometimes mistakes are made in surgery, in diagnosis, or in prescribing or administering drugs, resulting in ailments which are called **IATROGENIC**, caused by a physician or by a hospital.

© 2003 J&J Lundquist

# medicus

**[MEH di koos]    physician**

medicine – any substance used in treatment of disease or illness
medicinal – having the properties of a medicine; curative; remedial
medical – pertaining to the science or practice of medicine
medication – use or application of medicine
medicine man – person believed to possess magical curative powers, especially among North American Indians; a shaman
medicine ball – a solid, heavy, leather-covered ball tossed for exercise
Medicare – a U.S. government program of medical insurance for aged or disabled persons

**TEACHING NOTES:**   Throughout history, the field of **MEDICINE** has had its ups and downs. It has attracted those whose altruistic concern for their fellow man, like the Good Samaritan's, has prompted them to give care and healing to people who are sick, wounded, disabled, or troubled in any way.

Insurance companies have built large businesses to help people afford the increasingly expensive treatments that have become available through the remarkable advances in **MEDICAL** technology.

Societies in all parts of the world have had healers, **MEDICINE MEN,** or shamans. Sometimes these people functioned more as priests or representatives of the gods of the society than as medical healers. Others became doctors (from the Latin **DOCERE**—to teach) studying the science of ailments and how to cure them. They studied the various parts of the human body to find out how it might function free of aches, pains, or disease. In the past hundred years, much government and private money has been spent for medical research.

A large part of the field of **MEDICINE** in modern times has been devoted to learning how people should live in order to remain healthy and active and how to avoid such harmful practices as smoking, drinking to excess, eating too much fatty food, taking harmful drugs, or failing to exercise. Persuading people to live in a way that will help to prevent disease in the first place is a worthy endeavor. Perhaps students could create lists for themselves of their healthy habits and not-so-healthy habits, and make a plan of action for replacing the not-so-healthy habits with behaviors which would help them live healthier and happier lives.

© 2003 J&J Lundquist

LATIN

# sanus

**[SAH noos]   healthy, not diseased or injured**
sane – of sound or healthy mind
sanity – mental health or soundness
insane (in L. - not) – mentally ill or abnormal, not of healthy mind
insanity (in L. - not) – condition of mental illness
sanitarium – institution for treating the ill or insane; a health resort
sanitary – clean and healthy
sanitation – state of clean, healthy conditions

**TEACHING NOTES:** A Latin dictionary defines the Latin adjective, **SANUS**, as healthy, sound, not diseased or injured. Over the years, the idea of **SANITY** and **INSANITY** have come to suggest *mental* as opposed to *physical* well-being. While mankind has always valued cleanliness (more or less), it was when scientists began to study germs and bacteria and their relation to health and disease that **SANITATION** became a matter for modern governments to take seriously. Collecting garbage, sweeping the streets, outlawing litter, and providing sewage systems and storm drainage became government concerns. Today these activities are directed by the "Department of **SANITATION**." In Shel Silverstein's ***Where The Sidewalk Ends***, we find his classic poem *"The Sad Tale of Sara Cynthia Sylvia Stout"*—who would not take the garbage out. The poem helps children imagine what life would be like if the trash we generate daily were never removed from our houses. The poem is just right for reading aloud, illustrating, or memorizing! A class visit from the school custodian or a neighborhood garbage collector or "**SANITATION** engineer" might encourage more student understanding of the problem and respect for their local trash collectors.

People in cities and, later, in rural areas began to spend the family wealth on indoor plumbing for toilets, bathtubs, washing machines, etc. Public-spirited people provided **SANITARIUMS** (the Latin plural is really **SANITARIA**) to separate the sick from the germs of everyday life, and to prevent the ill from harming the public if their illness was contagious or caused dangerous behavior.

The Roman writer Juvenal wrote the famous phrase *"mens sana in corpore sano"*—a healthy mind in a healthy body. Students could write interesting papers explaining exactly what he meant by those words! Why not let them try?

© 2003 J&J Lundquist

GREEK

'ολος

# holos

**[HOH loss]    whole, entire, complete**

whole – healthy, unhurt, entire, total
hologram – three-dimensional picture of a whole object or whole person
catholic (kata G. - concerning, in respect of) – universal; applicable to all men; the universal church, or the whole body of Christians
holy – sacred; dedicated to the service of God, the church, or religion
holiday – a day fixed by law or custom to commemorate an event or to honor a person; day to honor religious saints or sacred events
holocaust (kaustos G. - burnt) – complete devastation or destruction by fire

**TEACHING NOTES:** Although our English words **WHOLE** (entire, complete) and **HOLE** (cavity, hollow place) sound alike, their nearly opposite definitions indicate different ancestry. The idea of a **WHOLE** is easy for most children to grasp, long before they learn to read. By studying fractions children learn the many ways in which a whole can be divided and possibly shared. Why not share a pizza or some other treat to solidify this concept? Some credit cards feature **HOLOGRAMS** as proof of their authenticity. Many students may be familiar with examples of holograms from the *Star Wars* movies.

Before the Reformation of the **CATHOLIC** Church, the term **catholic** (not capitalized) referred universally to all Christians. To some children, a **HOLIDAY** simply means a day off from school. When children learn that holidays originated as holy days and were intended as days of worship and gratitude, they gain a notion of the seriousness of thought and national values involved in the establishment of our secular holidays, such as Veteran's Day. Learning about holy days that are celebrated by different religions is important in teaching the principles of mutual respect and religious freedom so essential to our democracy. The original meaning of **HOLOCAUST** (a burnt offering) has evolved to suggest nuclear devastation or mass murder. The **HOLOCAUST**, when capitalized, refers to the heinous attempt by Adolf Hitler's Nazi regime to wipe out the entire population of Jewish people in Europe during WWII.

**EXTRA WORDS:** **HEAL**, to make whole or free from defect or disease, and **HEALTH**, soundness of body or mind, may not be direct descendants from the root **HOLOS**, (both spelled with *ea* instead of an *o*), but they are perhaps not-too-distant cousins. The Indo-European word *Qoilos* (whole) spawned both the Greek word *holos* and the Old High German word *heil*, which generated the Old English *hælin* (meaning healthy, whole). Teaching children to take responsibility for their **HEALTH** and to lead a **HEALTHY** life by choosing nutritious foods and exercising can produce lifelong benefits.

© 2003 J&J Lundquist

GREEK

ῥινος

# rhinos

**[HREE noss, REYE noss]   nose; snout**

**rhinoceros** (<u>keras</u> G. - horn) – large animal with one or two horns on its snout

**rhinocerotoid** – like a rhinoceros; one of the rhinoceros family

**rhinology** (<u>logos</u> G. - study, Vol. I, p. 15) – branch of medicine concerned with the nose

**rhinoplasty** (<u>plassein</u> G. - to form or mold) – plastic surgery for the nose

**rhinoscope** (<u>skopein</u> G. - to see, look, Vol. I, p. 13) – instrument for examining the interior of the nose

**TEACHING NOTES:** The **RHINOCEROS**, a large, heavy, thick-skinned, plant-eating mammal, lives in the warm tropical climates of Asia and Africa. When biologists named the animal, they chose to highlight its most unique characteristics, the very large nose and the one or two horns which decorate it. Its size and appearance are similar to the hippopotamus, or river horse (see **HIPPOS**, p.6), but oddly enough, the encyclopedia claims a "hippo" is related to the hog family. Should it have been called a "porcopotamus"? The **RHINOCEROS**, however, is more closely related to the horse! Maybe the real-life **RHINOCEROS**, an endangered species, dreamed of becoming the beautiful, mythical unicorn.

It is fun to decipher the Latin and Greek words invented by scientists for animals and plants back when Latin was used all over the world as the language for scientific discovery and comparison. The translations are often simple, e.g., **tyrannosaurus**–terrible lizard; **grandifloria**–big flowers.

*The Oxford English Dictionary* lists many specialized medical terms for various problems involving the nose. They all use the Greek word **RHINOS**, so knowing this word will help you know what part of the body is being discussed, e.g., **rhinencephalon** (rye-nen-SEF-a-lon).

**Rhinencephalon** (**kephale** G. - head) refers to the section of the brain where smell is processed. Want more? In plain English, **rhinencephalon** is the "olfactory lobe" (from the Latin word **OLFACERE** meaning "to smell" and the Greek word **LOBOS** meaning the *rounded part* or *division of an organ* such as the liver, lungs, brain, etc.). Oh! And don't forget ear **lobes**, and **tri*lob*ites**, those endearing but extinct, three-lobed, swimming creatures from early geologic eras. Ah, but that's a story for another day!

© 2003 J&J Lundquist

# cornu

### [KOR noo]    horn

cornet – horn, a brass instrument like a trumpet
cornucopia (copia L. - plenty; abundance) – horn of plenty
unicorn (unus L. - one) – a mythical horse with one horn on its forehead
corn – hardening of skin on a toe other than the toenail
cornea – the relatively hard, transparent coating of the eyeball that covers the iris and pupil and admits light to the interior of the eye

**TEACHING NOTES:** The Latin word **CORNU** is related to the Greek word **KERAS**, meaning an animal's horn. The Romans did not use the Greek letter Kappa (our letter K). They changed the *kappa* in Greek words to C. Consequently, some of our derivatives from the Greek language are spelled with a C. (Don't forget: C followed by e, i, or y is pronounced "s.") **TRICERATOPS** [tri (three) cerat (horn) ops (face)] means "three-horned face," which that well-known dinosaur clearly had! And, of course, **RHINOCEROS** [rhino (nose) ccra (horn)] meaning "horned nose" is familiar to all of us.

Our word **KERATIN**—referring to the fibrous protein epidermis (skin) found in horns, hooves, fingernails, toenails, and hair—has a number of derivative words rarely used outside of an ophthalmologist's or a dermatologist's clinic, such as **keratitis** (corneal inflammation), **keratoplasty** (corneal surgery), and **keratosis** (skin with an overgrowth of horn-like tissue).

The Latin word **CORNU** has some derivatives which relate to the *shape* of an animal's horn. A **CORNUCOPIA**, for example, is a large animal horn filled with fruit, grain, etc., and is used to suggest a plentiful harvest. Animal horns were used as the first musical wind instruments. A **CORNET** is a brass instrument with a shape like an animal horn. The shape was devised to make sounds similar to those of the ancient animal horn but more varied and vibrant.

Since our fingernails and toenails are hardened to protect the more fragile epidermis and are similar in composition to the animal's horns, hooves, and claws, they are relatively impervious to pain. The **CORNS** on a person's foot develop in response to painful rubbing or friction and so they form a protective layer to stop the pain. The **CORNEA** of the eye protects the eye from injury, from dust, or other invaders. The **KERATIN** content of those parts of the body provides the protection.

© 2003 J&J Lundquist

GREEK

δερμα

# derma

### [DAIR mah, DER mah]   skin, hide, shell

**dermis** – layer of skin just under the epidermis
**epidermis** (epi G. - upon) – outer layer of skin
**hypodermic** (hypo G. - under) – under the skin
**dermatologist** (logos G. - word, study, Vol. I, p. 15) – skin specialist in medicine
**dermatitis** (-itis G. - suffix – inflammation) – inflammation of the skin
**dermatoid** – skin-like
**dermoptera** (pteron G. - wing) – having skin or membranous wings like a bat

**TEACHING NOTES:** Our English word *skin* comes from the Middle English "skynn" and the Old Norse "skinn," and *they* got their words for skin from an old Greek word "schinden" (σχινδεν) meaning "peel" which is so old, it isn't even in our *Liddell & Scott Greek Lexicon*! (It *is*, however, cited in *Webster's Unabridged Dictionary, Second Edition*, which seems to have gone out of print– good luck finding one!) Those old English and old Norse folk used a lot of skins and furs which they "peeled" from animals. When skin doctors, **DERMATOLOGISTS**, began to study human skin, they thought they would upgrade their vocabulary by using Greek and Latin roots to create words for the new knowledge they were gaining.

The **DERMA** or *skin* is a fascinating organ of the human body. Drawing a diagram of the outer and inner layers, including the **subcutaneous** (see p. 40, **CUTIS** L. - skin) layers, where the hair follicles and sweat glands originate, would help children understand just why knee and elbow pads are a good idea when riding a bike or skateboard. They may want to find out what has to happen for cuts or abrasions to heal and look like new again. Looking at the **EPIDERMIS** of one's hand or arm with a good magnifying glass or microscope for the first time is almost always a revelation for a child!

A snake sheds its skin about three times a year. First, he rubs his nose on a rock or rough tree trunk to break a hole in his outgrown "straitjacket" and then wriggles out head first. The tail, still attached, is pulled through the old skin and finally comes out the former head end, breaks off, and the old skin is abandoned, inside out! And so the snake gets over his bad case of "**derma-*too*-titis**."

© 2003 J&J Lundquist

# cutis

### [KOO tis]    skin, hide

**cutis** – the layer of skin beneath the epidermis; derma

**cutis vera** (vera L. - true) – true skin; the layer of skin containing its blood supply and nerves

**subcutis** (sub L. - under) – the deeper or inner portion of the true skin

**cuticle** – thin, outermost thin layer of skin; the epidermis

**cuticula, cuticulae** – tough outer layer of skin in lower organisms (slugs, worms, etc.)

**cutaneous** – belonging to the skin; affecting the skin

**sub-cutaneous** (sub L. - under) – being used or introduced beneath the skin

**cutify** – to form skin

**TEACHING NOTES:**   The surface of hot chocolate cooling in a mug or of paint in an open can may be said to **CUTIFY**, but the term really refers to human or animal skin formation.

While we have given **DERMA** as the Greek word and **CUTIS** as the Latin word for "skin," the Romans themselves actually took **CUTIS** from another Greek word, **KUTOS** (κυτος), which also meant *skin* but more often referred to the hide of an animal that was used for leather, clothing, shoes, shields, etc.

The Greek word **KUTOS** evolved from the old Indo-European word for hides and leathers, "**SKU**," which the early Greeks pronounced **SKUTOS**. Some people then dropped the "*s*" sound and said **KUTOS**. The ancients seemed more concerned with the skin of animals for leather and for warmth and protection than they did for human skin. A scientific examination of human skin came later. Those old Indo-Europeans invented many words. They traveled to, and settled in, new lands, so the descendant words of their language are found from India (Sanskrit), all through Europe, and up into Scandinavia. Can you see the similarity between the modern Norwegian word "sko" for "shoe" and the Indo-European word "SKU" for hide and leather?

Someone is sure to ask about our slang word "cute." It is not from **CUTIS**. It is a short form of "acute" from the Latin **ACUTUS**, meaning sharp.

© 2003 J&J Lundquist

# cor cordis

### [KOR, KOR dis]   heart

core – the central or innermost part; the "heart" of anything

cordial – heartfelt; warm and sincere

courage (n.) – facing danger in spite of fear

encourage (in L. - in, within) – to give confidence to; to inspire with courage

discourage (dis L. - apart) – to dishearten

accord (ad L. - to, toward, Vol. I, p. 20) – heart to heart; an agreement or a treaty

concord (con from cum L. - with, Vol. I, p. 23) – agreement between people; harmony in music

discord (dis L. - apart) – disagreement or conflict; harsh or inharmonious noise in music

record (re L. - again) – to preserve the heart of a message

**TEACHING NOTES:** Anyone who has had his or her feelings hurt or his character insulted might say (somewhat dramatically) that he was "wounded to the **CORE**" meaning "to the heart." Our word **COURAGE** came to us from Latin via French, in which the word for heart is "**COEUR**."

It is ironic to think that one of the first battles in the American Revolution was fought in a little town in Massachussetts called **CONCORD**, a name which means agreement and harmony. If the students have not heard the story of the important events at Lexington and **CONCORD**, they would enjoy hearing Henry Wadsworth Longfellow's poem *"Paul Revere's Ride."* Some may even be **ENCOURAGED** to commit it to memory! Perhaps the most **COURAGEOUS** ones in the class will want to recite the poem to an audience. Memorizing poetry of any kind is a valuable activity.

**RECORD** is one of the many words that can be a noun or a verb, based on where the speaker puts the accent. If the accent is on the first syllable, as in **rec´-ord**, the word is a noun and refers to a written or otherwise preserved piece of information or music. **Re-cord´**, on the other hand, means to preserve information, music, or video by any of various **RE-CORD´-ING** methods. *The Guinness Book of Records* is a vast fund of **RECORDED** information. In 1954, Roger Bannister became the first man to run a mile in under four minutes, a feat that many had thought humanly impossible. Since then, several others have broken his world **RECORD**. Many great things have been done by people who refused to be **DISCOURAGED** when others told them their goals were unachievable.

© 2003 J&J Lundquist

LATIN

# dorsum

**[DOR soom]   back**

**dorsal fin** – the fin on the back of sharks, dolphins, orca, and some fish
**endorse** (v.) – to sign on the back of a document or check; support
**endorsement** (n.) – signature written on the back of a check; support or approval for a person or position or product
**dorsicumbent** (incumbo L. - lie upon, lean toward) – lie upon one's back
**dorsigerous** (gerere L. - to carry) – carrying the young on the back
**dossier** (*French*) – a bundle of documents labeled on the back

**TEACHING NOTES:** The **DORSAL FIN** of the friendly bottlenose dolphin often causes this gentle creature to be mistaken for a shark when the rest of the body is concealed under water. The **DORSAL FIN** and "saddle patch" (grey blotches behind the dorsal fin) of orca, a.k.a. killer whales, are as individual as fingerprints and are used to identify different pod members. The **DORSAL FINS** of orcas in captivity flop over. We couldn't find an explanation for this. Any ideas why?

In order to deposit a check in the bank, one has to **ENDORSE** it by signing it on the **back**. If the check is made out to you, you are the **ENDORSEE**. Some companies pay large sums of money to athletes or celebrities to **ENDORSE** (show approval of) their products. The implied message is that, if you use the same product as this famous person, you may achieve the same level of success in sports or other areas. Some celebrities make more money from **ENDORSEMENTS** than they do from their regular activities. Have students think of celebrities and the products they **ENDORSE** and ask them why a company would choose that celebrity to advertise that particular product. When children are aware of how advertising aims at creating a desire for a certain item, they are less easily fooled by dubious promises. Political candidates also receive **ENDORSEMENTS** from people who contribute to their campaigns or who support them.

After a story or a trip to the zoo to meet some **DORSIGEROUS** (dor-SI-jer-ous) animals such as opossums or koalas, who often transport their young on their **backs**, the class might spread out a cloth on the grass and munch cookies and milk while **DORSICUMBENTLY** watching the changing shapes of the passing clouds. (One doesn't meet these unusual words every day, but as they say, use them three times in conversation and they will be yours!)

A **DOSSIER** (doss´ e a) is a file containing detailed records on a person or subject. The French coined the word because the file was labeled on the **back**. Police departments, intelligence agencies, companies, schools, all keep **DOSSIERS** about the various people they are interested in. Perhaps students would like to assemble personal dossiers with their own important papers, examples of writing, drawing, school records, or letters.

© 2003 J&J Lundquist

GREEK

αθλο ν

# athlon

**[AHT lohn]   prize, award**

athlete – a person trained or skilled in exercises, sports, or games requiring physical strength, agility, or stamina
athletics – exercises, games, or sports engaged in by athletes
athletic – characteristic of an athlete; pertaining to athletics
pentathlon (penta G. - five) – athletic contest of five separate sports
decathlon (deka G. - ten) – athletic contest of ten separate sports
decathlete – an athlete who participates in a decathlon

**TEACHING NOTES:**   The ancient Greeks were intensely competitive. The idea underlying the word **ATHLON** was prize or award and the related verb, **ATHLEIN**, meant to compete for a prize. The Greeks greatly admired and celebrated **ATHLETES**. They were more interested in individual contests than in team sports. There was less emphasis on timing and records than on who could beat whom! The defense of a Greek city-state involved battles that were fought primarily by wielding swords and shields in close combat or by throwing spears and javelins. **ATHLETIC** skills tended to be those that had to be developed for military combat and for the protection of one's home or city-state.

The Greeks started the Olympic Games early in the 8th century B.C., 776 B.C. to be exact, and continued them every four years until 393 A.D., when they were abolished by the militant Christian Emperor Theodosius I. Students should note that when we talk about B.C. dates, we count *backwards* from the year 0—zero (the year of the birth of Christ)—so the years before the birth were 1 B.C., 2 B.C., and so on. In a time line, 776 B.C. actually comes BEFORE 708 B.C., which was approximately when the Greeks at Olympia added jumping, discus throwing, javelin throwing, and wrestling to the foot races.

Use your local playing field as the venue for a class-wide Olympic Games celebration to create a memorable experience. Participating in some of the original events such as foot races, discus throwing, and javelin throwing helps to bring the ancient games to life. A very nice discus can be improvised by using two Frisbees, filled with sand and duct-taped together. Students can wear something resembling the ancient Greek chitons or tunics (find pictures by typing [Greek + chiton] into an internet search engine). Winners may receive a crown of laurel or oak leaves. There should, of course, be a celebratory feast featuring Greek food such as olives, grapes, dolmas, feta cheese, grape juice, figs, dates, and bread.

Perhaps someone could report to the class on how the modern **PENTATHLON** differs from the ancient version. The **DECATHLON** is a modern track-and-field competition featuring ten events. Bruce Jenner is a famous **DECATHLETE**.

© 2003 J&J Lundquist

GREEK

αγων

# agon

### [AH gon]   contest, struggle, trial

**agony** – intense mental or physical suffering from struggling with a challenge or problem

**agonize** – to suffer agony, or anguish over a decision

**antagonize** (anti L. - against) – to act in opposition to; to incur or provoke hostility; to struggle against

**antagonist** – one who struggles against or opposes another; adversary; opponent

**antagonism** – actively expressed opposition or hostility; enmity

**protagonist** (pro L. - for) – principal character in a book or play against which antagonistic forces struggle

**TEACHING NOTES:** Although the words **AGON** and **ATHLOS** both mean "a contest," they have different connotations. **ATHLOS** calls up images of the joy of **ATHLETICS** and the pleasure of **ATHLETES** who are fit to compete in the Olympic Games, whereas **AGON** suggests the **AGONY** of struggle such as that seen on the faces of professional wrestlers whom many watch on television.

In the great Greek dramas, the hero contends with or fights against those who oppose him. The hero is the **PROTAGONIST** and the villains who are against him are the **ANTAGONISTS**. Students might enjoy reporting on dramas they have watched on television, giving a brief explanation of what the conflict or contest was all about. Or perhaps the whole class could read a play aloud, identify the **PROTAGONIST** and the **ANTAGONIST**, discover why they are opposing each other, and predict how the struggle will be resolved by the end of the play. This would be excellent preparation for a lifetime of theatre-going!

Of course, in all sports the team one is cheering for becomes the **PROTAGONISTS**, and the opposing team the **ANTAGONISTS**. In sports, however, unlike in dramas, neither side is necessarily "the bad guy." As long as good sportsmanship is observed by all the contestants, all have to recognize that without worthy opponents who are willing to risk "the **AGONY** of defeat," there would be no game and no glory!

© 2003 J&J Lundquist

GREEK

δρομος

# dromos

**[DROH moss]   race course, runway, running**
hippodrome (hippos G. - horse) – horse racetrack
dromedary – a camel of unusual speed
anadromous (ana G. - up) – running upward
catadromous (kata G. - down) – running downward
aerodrome (aer G. - air) – airport runway
palindrome (palin G. - back, again) – a word, sentence, or verse that
    reads the same backward or forward

**TEACHING NOTES:**   Because the Greeks and Romans loved horse races, they built **HIPPODROMES** with seats for spectators where such races could be staged. The Circus Maximus at the foot of the Palatine Hill in Rome was the scene of many horse and chariot races. The film ***Ben Hur*** has wonderful depictions of such chariot races that would be well worth showing to students.

**DROMEDARY** (DROM-eh-derry) refers to a camel trained to be ridden fast. Now it is the name for an Arabian, single-humped camel. Sometimes you can see pictures of dromedaries on packages of dates, exported from the Arab world.

We, who eat salmon and other fish which fight their way up rivers and streams to spawn, do our best to protect our **ANADROMOUS** (a-NAD-ro-mous) fish populations. And, of course, those same fish in their earlier years are **CATADROMOUS**, because they swim downstream to the ocean to live their adult lives in salt water until they are ready to swim back upstream to their home in order to spawn and then to die. The life of an **ANADROMOUS** and **CATADROMOUS** fish definitely has its *ups* and *downs*!

**AERODROME** is an early British term for a place for airplanes to take off, land, and be stored. In the modern world of huge, complex airports, the term **AERODROME** seems quaint. It suggests intrepid barnstorming aviators in leather helmets, goggles, and white silk scarves flying single-motor, open-cockpit biplanes such as those flown by WWI pilots or the Red Baron. It is hard to imagine the changes in the aerospace industry since the Wright brothers first became airborne in 1903. There are usually several students fascinated by the history of aviation and willing to share their knowledge.

**PALINDROMES** are words or sentences in which the letters are the same backward or forward. Bob, Hannah, Eve, and Mom are **PALINDROMIC** names. Here are some sentences in which the letters are the same backward or forward. For example, in "dontnod" or "olsonisinoslo" or "ilovemevoli," punctuation creates meaning: *"Don't nod," "Olson is in Oslo," "I Love Me, Vol. I," "Was it a car or a cat I saw?" "Able was I ere I saw Elba."* Have fun making up your own and finding more on the Internet!

© 2003 J&J Lundquist

# mons montis

### [MONS, MOHN tis] mountain

**mountain** – a land mass that rises high above its surroundings
**mountainous** – terrain containing many mountains
**mount** – to rise, ascend; to place or seat oneself upon something
**mound** – a raised area in the ground
**insurmountable** (in L. - not; sur L. - above) – something one cannot rise above
**amount** – a pile or accumulation of anything; the quantity at hand
**promontory** (pro L. - forward) – a high point of land projecting into a body of water; mass of land projecting into a lowland
**paramount** (para L. - by) – superior to or rising above all others

**TEACHING NOTES:** MOUNTAINS were very important to the old Romans. When people of the ancient world looked for a good place to build a town, they had to find a location close to a water supply with a hill that could be fortified and defended. No wonder they chose ROME! Rome had seven hills and the Tiber River ran at the foot of them. The Tiber River, however, begins in the Apennine MOUNTAINS, descends 250 miles, and enters the Tyrrhenian Sea at Ostia. Its rapid descent caused it to churn up silt, making the water a "tawny brown" color when it got to Rome. In the hot months of the year, it was not very refreshing to drink! The resourceful Romans, however, built aqueducts, bringing fresh, cool water from MOUNTAIN streams. In the steamiest months, wealthy Romans vacationed on the coast near Pompeii.

MOUNTAINS were symbols of strength and permanence but were also something to be feared. Volcanic MOUNTAINS shaped the environment of both Italy and Greece. The volcanic MOUNTAIN, Vesuvius, erupted in 79 A.D., spewing hot ash which buried the beautiful little coastal cities of Pompeii and Herculaneum, thus preserving a perfect record of the Roman way of life. Homes, stores, theatres, people, and animals were suddenly encased in fine, powdery ash which preserved the paintings on the walls, the food on the tables, and even the agonized expressions on people's faces as they tried to escape.

Diamond Head is a well-known **PROMONTORY** on the island of Oahu in Hawaii. It is an extinct volcano and is not **INSURMOUNTABLE**. Many people climb into its crater to visit the National Guard Base which is situated there. Asking permission beforehand is of **PARAMOUNT** importance!

© 2003 J&J Lundquist

LATIN

# humus

**[HOO moos]   earth, soil**

humus – dark organic matter in soils partially containing decomposed vegetable or animal material
humiliate – to make someone feel low
humble – near the ground; not high or pretentious
humility – a spirit of lowliness; lack of pretension
humification – formation of humus

**TEACHING NOTES:** Ed Hume, host of a TV gardening advice program, has an ideal name, since he recommends **HUMUS** to his listeners on a regular basis. On the earth's crust, soil is formed by the disintegration of bedrock that has flaked off, weathered, and become pulverized. It is standard practice to add **HUMUS**, made in a compost bin, to the soil to make one's garden a rich growing medium! Students might like to construct compost bins at home and then add grass clippings, leaves, and other organic material, as well as some hard-working earthworms. They will be pleased to see what rich humus they can create with which to enrich their own flower or vegetable gardens. Any library or the Internet will have directions on how to build a compost bin.

To make people feel low or inadequate by embarrassing them is to **HUMILIATE** them, or to make them literally "feel like dirt." Someone who is **HUMILIATED** is sometimes referred to as having to "eat **HUMBLE** pie." This phrase evolved from "umble pie," a venison pie made from certain inferior parts of a deer and usually served to underlings, while the better-tasting and more tender pieces were reserved for the masters of the estate.

To be truly **HUMBLE** is to recognize the lack of importance of one's own successes and not to believe that one is better than others. To **HUMBLE** someone else is to bring a person "down to earth" if he or she is feeling a little too impressed with himself or herself. Someone with **HUMILITY** is someone who does not brag about his own accomplishments and does not treat others as inferior if they have not reached the same level of achievement. Good sportsmanship demands that one be quick to acknowledge the role others have played in his or her success. It is always interesting to listen to the talk of star athletes who are being interviewed on television after a team victory to see whether they are vainglorious and take all the credit for themselves or whether they speak **HUMBLY** and give credit to their teammates.

© 2003 J&J Lundquist

LATIN

# folium

**[FO lee oom]   leaf**

foliage – the leaves of a plant or tree
folio – a leaf of paper (either loose or in a bound volume)
portfolio (porto L. - carry) – a case for carrying loose sheets of paper, music, art, etc.
foliate – to put forth leaves; to beat metal into a thin leaf or foil
exfoliate (ex L. - away from) – to cast off or shed leaves or layers
defoliate (de L. - down from) – to strip off leaves
defoliant – a chemical used to cause defoliation

**TEACHING NOTES:** Is there a connection between the earliest paper that was made in Egypt from the papyrus plant found near the Nile River and the fact that we speak of writing on "leaves of paper?" Making paper is a marvelously satisfying project for a classroom. Many library books give instructions on how to do it. Writing or drawing on this precious paper can create a family heirloom!

When man discovered that his skin grew in thin layers (think of how sunburned skin peels), it was natural to think of these paper-thin layers as similar to the pages of a book. When one wants to renew one's skin, one can apply lotions which will aid in the **EXFOLIATION** of old, rough, damaged skin and reveal the new soft layer of skin beneath it.

The **DEFOLIATION** of the leaves of a tree is sometimes done by a swarm of migratory, short-horned grasshoppers called locusts or cicadas, who arrive and eat all the leaves of the trees in a neighborhood and then move on. They are more likely to appear in some parts of the country than in others. Some of them come out only every 17 years—and are known as "17-Year Locusts." They are mentioned in the Bible as one of the plagues. Is there a history of locust visits in your part of the country?

Deciduous trees lose their **FOLIAGE** in the fall, but evergreens keep their needles all year round. In those parts of the world which have clearly defined seasons, there is shade-giving **FOLIAGE** on trees in summer months. Vibrantly colorful **FOLIAGE** appears in the fall. In winter, **DEFOLIATION** leaves the tree limbs starkly outlined against the sky. Finally, each returning spring brings tiny, swelling, green buds, making tree **FOLIAGE** silently responsible for the changing states of mind of many of the world's people. Thoughtful students may want to write an essay or poem to reflect on this recurring aspect of our lives.

© 2003 J&J Lundquist

LATIN

# sal
# salis

### [SAHL, SAH lis]    salt

**salt** – a substance which occurs in nature both in solution and in crystalline form, known chemically as sodium chloride (NaCl)

**salary** – fixed payment made periodically to a person for regular work

**saline** – like salt; salty

**salami** – variety of sausage highly salted and flavored, originally Italian

**desalinate** (de L. - away from) – to remove salt from water or land

**saltern** – a building where salt is made by boiling or evaporating sea water

**salinometer** (metron G. - measure) – an instrument for measuring the amount of salt in a solution

**TEACHING NOTES:**   Since **SALT** is essential to human life and health, it has always been a valuable commodity. Sometimes it was even used as money. Roman soldiers and other workers received part of their pay in salt which was called a **SALARIUM** (the source of our word **SALARY**). The Roman soldiers even built a special military road, the *Via Salaria* (or *"Salt Way"*), from Rome to the **SALT WORKS** at Ostia, where **SALT** was produced by evaporating seawater. Common **SALT**, also called table **SALT**, which we use to season food, has many other uses including preserving food, processing leather, even freezing ice cream. Anyone who has tasted his or her own tears knows that tears have a salty flavor. People who wear contact lenses rinse them in a **SALINE** solution, because it is **SALTY** like the natural moisture in their eyes.

There is more fascinating information in encyclopedias and on the Internet about the history and uses of **SALT** than you would ever expect. Perhaps a team of researchers could take on a project about **SALT** and give a report to the class. Pour some **SALT** on black paper and look at it through a microscope. You will see perfect tiny cubes. No machine makes them. **SALT** crystals come that way naturally. Compare the salt crystals to granules of sugar under the microscope and don't forget to compare the taste! Has anyone in class ever tasted a batch of cookies in which salt was substituted for sugar by mistake? What a disappointment! However, when something is expected to be **SALTY**, such as **SALAMI**, we appreciate the **SALTY** flavor.

Some ships carry **DESALINIZATION** machines to convert **SALTY** seawater into clear drinking water. This way, they can take longer voyages before having to visit a port to take on fresh water.

An old sailor is sometimes referred to as an "old **SALT**."

© 2003 J&J Lundquist

LATIN

# mare

**[MAH reh]    sea, ocean**

marine – (adj.) of, or relating to, the sea; (noun) a sea-soldier
marina – a dock or basin offering safe mooring for boats
mariner – a person who navigates a ship; a sailor
maritime – of, or relating to, navigation or commerce on the sea
submarine (sub L. - under) – ship which goes under water in the ocean
mare nostrum – "our sea"; a body of water belonging to one nation or shared by two or more nations; the Romans' name for the Mediterranean Sea

**TEACHING NOTES:** Even before Homer's time, the seas and oceans provided important routes for trade between nations and cultures, and inspired countless stories. *The Odyssey* is one of Western civilization's oldest stories of adventures on the sea. Other **MARITIME** adventures include *Kidnapped* and *Treasure Island* by Robert Louis Stevenson, the *Hornblower* series by C. S. Forester, and *The Boy Who Sailed Around the World Alone* by Robin Lee Graham. All over the world there are **MARITIME** museums which feature famous sailing ships and local boating history. Perhaps the most famous **MARITIME** museum is in Greenwich, England, outside London, where Greenwich Mean Time (GMT) provides the anchor for the twenty-four time zones around the world.

A visit to an aquarium always provides a fascinating glimpse into the world of **MARINE** life. The study of the interdependence of **MARINE** creatures and humans can help children grow up to be responsible stewards of their environment. Near an aquarium one may find a **MARINA**, where boats can tie up to a dock and be sheltered from rough waves.

The **MARINES**, an elite branch of the U.S. military, are concerned with operations on water or on land. **MARINES** are often the first forces on site in a battle in order to secure the area for army and naval forces to arrive. The logo of the Seattle **MARINERS** baseball team includes the points of a compass, such as one a **MARINER** would use to navigate the seas.

Any child can understand that a hollow bathtub toy can't sink without a little hole to let water into the toy. The same principle explains a **SUBMARINE'S** ability to submerge. Children might want to research the process of how ballast tanks allow **SUBMARINES** to remain just below the surface of the water, at periscope depth, and to dive deep in the ocean. Some say that attacks by German **SUBS**, called U-Boats (*Unterseebooten*), on neutral ships like the *Lusitania* lured the United States into WWI.

**EXTRA WORDS:** *Mal de mer* is a French term meaning seasickness.

© 2003 J&J Lundquist

**GREEK**

ναυς

# naus

**[NAH oos]   ship, boat**

nautical – pertaining to ships
aeronaut (aero G. - air) – an early name for an aviator; airplane pilot
astronaut (astron G. - star, Vol. I, p. 63) – one who "sails" out toward the stars
cosmonaut (kosmos G. - ordered universe) – astronaut
nautilus – a sea creature which forms new chambers in a spiral formation as it grows
nausea – seasickness caused by the motion of a boat
nauseate – to make sick with an upset stomach due to any cause
Argonauts – heroes in Greek mythology who sailed with Jason on his ship, the *Argo*, in search of the Golden Fleece

**TEACHING NOTES:**   Ancient Greece was a maritime land. The Greeks sailed among the islands close to their mainland and later all over the Mediterranean Sea. They built huge ships, sometimes stacked three decks high, called triremes. Naturally, Greek myths were often sea stories.

The Spartan King, Menelaus, had a beautiful wife, Helen, who was stolen away by Paris, the Prince of Troy. Furious, Menelaus and his brother, King Agamemnon of Mycenae, declared war on Troy. The Greeks gathered at Aulis and were delayed, awaiting favorable winds for their hundreds of ships. (Helen's beauty was so famous that her face is referred to as "the face that launched a thousand ships.") Agamemnon offered to sacrifice his daughter, Iphigenia, to placate the goddess Artemis, who was withholding the winds. However, a moment before the sacrifice, Artemis took pity on Iphigenia, rescued her, made her a priestess, and then caused the winds to blow once again. Then the Greek **NAUTICAL** expedition began.

The Greeks sailed to Troy where they besieged the city for ten years. They finally used treachery to get inside the high walls of Troy. They pretended to sail away, leaving behind a huge wooden horse (in which Greek soldiers were hiding). The Trojans pulled the amazing horse into their city. That night the soldiers crept out and opened the city gates to all the Greek warriors. The Greeks were finally able to destroy the city of Troy. King Menelaus then sailed home with Helen. The war was over. This is all explained and illustrated in the D'Aulaires' ***Book of Greek Myths***.

The symbolic characters in these myths, rich products of ancient Greek imagination, have worked their way into the literature of Western civilization. Children need to be familiar with the myths in order to understand references to them in their reading. The story of Jason, his ship, *Argo*, and the adventures of the **ARGONAUTS** is another myth beautifully told in the D'Aulaires' ***Book of Greek Myths***.

© 2003 J&J Lundquist

LATIN

# navis

### [NAH wis]   ship, boat

**navy** – the maritime section of a nation's defense; the ships and those who manage them

**naval** – pertaining to ships and those who build, sail, and manage them

**navigate** (ago L. - do, drive) – to determine the route a ship must take to a destination; to direct the course of a ship or any vehicle

**navigation** – the process of guiding a ship upon the sea

**navigable** – body of water deep enough to allow movement of ships

**circumnavigate** (circum L. - around) – to sail completely around a land mass or the world

**TEACHING NOTES:**   One of the most fascinating aspects of history is naval history, how, from earliest times, men have devised ways of traveling on water, **NAVIGATING** on rivers, lakes, and oceans. Primitive ways of floating safely on water by means of hollowed-out tree trunks, "bowl boats," canoes fashioned from skins, or birch bark stretched over wooden frames, show the great ingenuity of man and his fascination with crossing expanses of water too vast to bridge.

Students can research the development of **NAVIGATION**, by various means: landmarks, the stars, time pieces, and ever-more-accurate clocks; and later, by new ways of measuring speed of passage on the ocean, and most recently, satellites and GPS (Global Positioning Systems).

Students always enjoy studying famous seafaring explorers throughout history, such as the Minoans, the Carthaginians, the Phoenicians, the Greeks, the Romans, and the Vikings. A few great early explorers were Eric the Red and his son Leif Ericson (who sailed to America), Vitus Bering, Sebastian Cabot, Christopher Columbus, Sir Francis Drake, Henry Hudson, Ferdinand Magellan, Amerigo Vespucci, Vasco da Gama, Captain James Cook, and one of our favorites, a Portuguese prince known simply as Henry the **NAVIGATOR**. The boats and ships they **NAVIGATED** and where they traveled are worth the time of a student's own exploration. Perhaps one can find out which of these explorers **CIRCUMNAVIGATED** the world!

Someone may ask about the word *"nave,"* referring to the central body of a church extending from the main back entry to the choir in the front, and wonder how it relates to **NAVIS**. It does not. This word and *"navel,"* meaning belly button, derive from old German words meaning *middle* or *center*. They are not derived from **NAVIS**. The "e" in the spelling of "nave" and "navel" is the clue to the different meanings and is worth remembering.

© 2003 J&J Lundquist

GREEK

ʽομος

# homos

### [HOH moss]     same, common, joint

**homograph** (graphein G. - to write or draw, Vol. I, p. 2) – words with the same spelling but different origin and meaning

**homonym** (onyma G. - name) – words having the same sound or pronunciation but different spelling and meaning

**homogeneous** (genos G. - race, kind) – same kind or nature

**homogenize** – to make homogeneous or the same throughout

**homosexual** – erotic attraction for one of the same sex

**TEACHING NOTES:** **HOMOGRAPH** refers to words with the same spelling but different meanings, like *fair (market or festival); fair (beautiful or blond); bear (carry); bear (furry animal)*. **HOMONYMS**, on the other hand, sound alike but are spelled differently and have different meanings, like *bare–bear, fare–fair, there–their–they're; not–knot; hare–hair*. Can the students think of others? Learning a list of them can help a great deal in preventing spelling errors.

    **HOMOGENEOUS** is used to refer to a group of people having many qualities in common, such as national characteristics, history, race, etc. Many of the world's nations are **HOMOGENEOUS** because their people have lived in the same region for many generations. A German person is German because, as far back as he or she can trace, the family lived in Germany. French people are people whose ancestors have lived in France. Japanese people have Japanese ancestry. But some countries, like Australia and the United States, are becoming more **HETEROGENEOUS**, having citizens from all over the world (see **HETEROS**, p. 54).

    While the word **HOMOGENIZE** has been in use for a long time, it has come to refer principally to the process which gives milk a consistent texture by preventing its separation into skim milk and cream. Research on the Internet or in an encyclopedia could help a group of students explain to the class how the process of **HOMOGENIZATION** works! Skimming cream off fresh milk and churning that cream into butter the old-fashioned way can help students visualize what gets **HOMOGENIZED** into whole milk. Churning butter can also give students an appreciation for the time and effort people used to put into creating products, which we now take for granted, like butter. Numerous Internet sites give instructions for making fresh butter. A trip to a local dairy might help and would illuminate the related process of pasteurization and the many steps required to bring our vital milk supplies to our family tables.

© 2003 J&J Lundquist

GREEK

ἑτερος

# heteros

**[HEH teh ross]   other, different**

heterogeneous (<u>genos</u> G. - race, kind) – different kind or nature
heterodox (<u>doxa</u> G. - opinion) – contrary to recognized standard
   practice or doctrine (opposite of orthodox)
heterography (<u>graphein</u> G. - write, Vol. I, p. 2) – spelling different from
   that which is correct in current usage; incorrect spelling
heteronomy (<u>nomos</u> G. - law) – not self-governing (opposite of
   autonomy)
heterosexual – passion for one of the opposite sex

**TEACHING NOTES:** Turn to the page showing the Greek alphabet and look at the letters **eta** (pronounced "AY-tah") and **epsilon** (pronounced "EHP-si-lon"). These two letters are used for different sounds of our letter E. The capital form of **eta** looks like our letter "H", but is not pronounced like it. There is no letter "h" in Greek like our English letter "h." They did, however, pronounce the *sound* of the letter "h" on some of their words which began with a vowel. If *h* were to be sounded, the beginning vowel was written with a backward apostrophe ( ʽ ), called a "rough breathing mark," or over the second vowel if the word began with a diphthong, like ai, as in aisle. If no *h* sound were to be used, they used a "smooth breathing mark" (ʼ) written like a regular apostrophe. See if you can pronounce these words:
1. ʽομηρ;  2. ʽοριζον.  Hints: (1. an early Greek poet; 2. the line between sea and sky).

Some derivatives using **HETEROS**, meaning "different," have opposite terms using **HOMOS**, meaning "same." For example, *HETEROGENEOUS*, different kind, is the opposite of *HOMOGENEOUS*, same kind.

However, *HETERONOMY* (governed by other than oneself) is the opposite of *AUTONOMY* (governing oneself or being a law to oneself), and *HETERODOXY* (other than straight or traditional doctrine) is the opposite of *ORTHODOXY* (straight teaching or doctrine).

**HETEROGRAPHY** is a nice, respectful term for the kinds of spelling one often finds in the writings of early Americans like John and Abigail Adams, who wrote before spelling was as standardized as it is today. They often wrote to each other during stressful times, like the American Revolution. Their spelling is usually quite phonetic ("extreamly; Phyladelphia; politicks" in letters from John Adams to Abigail Adams and to Richard Cranch on Sept. 18, 1774, from *The Adams Papers: Series II—Adams Family Correspondence, Vol. I., 1963*) and can be deciphered easily, but it is, well, "**HETERO**."

© 2003 J&J Lundquist

LATIN

# cardo cardinis

**[KAR do, KAR di nis]   hinge**

cardinal – essential, main; a songbird with bright red feathers
cardinal numbers – one, two, three, etc.
cardinal points (on a compass) – North, South, East, West
cardinal winds – winds blowing from one of the cardinal points of the compass
cardinal edge (of a shell) – the connection between the two bivalves of a shell
Cardinal – one of 70 princes of the Roman Catholic Church

**TEACHING NOTES:** In English we use the old German word **hinge** (a derivative of **hang**) for the small but important device on which every door swings. Think how important **hinges** are in our world! Perhaps the students can locate some **hinges** in the classroom.

The original Latin word **CARDO** meaning a **hinge**, a small device on which a door is **hung** and swung, has come into English usage almost entirely as metaphor. Remember, a metaphor is a figure of speech in which one thing is likened to another different thing by being spoken of as if it were that other. E.g., "All the world's a stage."

For example, in debate, the **CARDINAL** points are the main ideas on which the whole argument *hinges*. **CARDINAL NUMBERS** are the counting numbers from one to ten on which the entire number system swings, or is built. A student with a compass may enjoy showing how to find the various points *between* the **CARDINAL POINTS**—North, South, East, and West (such as NNW, ESE, etc.). Students may also enjoy locating the school and their homes on a map and determining the directions they must travel to and from school. At the beach, one may find clam, scallop, or mussel shells which have a **CARDINAL EDGE,** the place where the two sides are joined by a pliable **hinge**.

**CARDINALS** of the Roman Catholic Church comprise the Pope's council of 6 **cardinal** bishops, 50 **cardinal** priests, and 14 **cardinal** deacons. These 70 men, on whom the government of the church **hinges**, elect a Pope from among themselves after a Pope's death. They wear robes of bright scarlet red.

What do birds have to do with **hinges**? The North American singing bird that we call a **CARDINAL**, *Cardinalis Virginianus*, was named because the color of the plumage of the male of the species resembled the red of the robes of the Catholic **CARDINALS**. Since these beautiful, bright red birds are common in the Midwest, the city of St. Louis, Missouri, named its Major League baseball team the **CARDINALS**.

© 2003 J&J Lundquist

LATIN

# porta

### [POR tah]   door, gate, entry

port – a harbor for boats at the shore of a city; the left side of a ship, as one faces forward; a place to connect pieces of computer hardware so they can communicate with each other

airport – a place where airplanes land and take off

portal – doorway or gateway of stately or elaborate construction; any kind of entryway

porthole – small opening in the side of a ship to let in light or air

porch – a covered area around the entrance to a house

portcullis – (Old French *coulies* - sliding) vertically sliding castle door

**TEACHING NOTES:**   *Webster's Collegiate Dictionary* ties the two roots (*porta* and *porto, portatum*) together through the derivative **PORTER**. While the most common meaning of porter is someone who carries something (from **PORTO**—to carry), the British also use the word **PORTER** for someone who stands next to a door to assist those who enter. Americans call this person a doorman.

The word **PORT** is a beautiful illustration of the metaphoric quality of English. Just as a **PORT** is a place to load and unload a ship, an **AIRPORT** is the place for planes to take on or deliver passengers and cargo. In the days when boats had a steering board on the right side, or starboard, it was easiest to pull up to a dock if you kept the dock (**PORT**) on the larboard, or left side of the boat. The use of the word **PORT**, instead of larboard, was adopted to avoid confusion when calling out directions in windy conditions. If one pictures a personal computer as a boat dock, and peripherals (printers, scanners, joysticks, etc.) as boats wanting to tie up to that dock, it's easy to see how the places to connect the cables came to be called **PORTS**. We often hear the word **PORTAL** refer to different gateways to the Internet, such as *MSN*, *AOL*, or *Yahoo*. Passing through one of these electronic doorways allows you to launch your voyage across the ocean of information on the Internet.

**PORTHOLES** are small openings, usually round or oval, that admit light into the sides of a ship. In the days of fighting sail, **PORTHOLES** were gun **PORTS**, which had doors which could be raised to allow a cannon barrel to slide out, fire, then be closed again against the weather.

A **PORTCULLIS** is a strong or heavy grating of horizontal and vertical bars of wood or iron. The vertical bars are pointed at the lower end and suspended by chains. The **PORTCULLIS** is constructed to slide up and down in vertical grooves on both sides of a gateway to a fortress or old castle. It can be let down quickly as a defense against an attack. Perhaps someone in class would like to build a working model. It would be great fun to take the model **PORTCULLIS** to the beach and build it into a sand castle!

© 2003 J&J Lundquist

LATIN

# porto
# portatum

### [POR to, por TAH toom]    to carry

porter – someone who carries your luggage for you

portable – capable of being carried by hand or in person

portage – (n.) the act of carrying anything;
  (v.) to carry a boat over land between two bodies of water

transport (trans L. - across, Vol. I, p. 55) – to carry across; to carry away with emotion

export (ex L. - out of) – to carry out; to send goods or info out

import (in L. - in) – (v.) to carry in; to bring something in

important – (adj.) carrying meaning or significance

report (re L. - back) – (v.) to carry back

support (sub L. - under) – (v.) carry from underneath; to bear

deport (de L. - away) – (v.) to carry away

**TEACHING NOTES:** All these **PORT** words—**TRANSPORT, EXPORT, IMPORT,** and **DEPORT**—call up misleading visual images of sending and receiving things from a harbor or port. This is why we placed these two words together, so the distinction can be made. **PORTO, PORTATUM** means *to carry* and all those prefixes simply say "carry across," "carry out," "carry in," and "carry away."

One may see **PORTERS** in hotels, where guests arrive with lots of bags. At airports they are usually referred to as skycaps. Laptop computers and palm pilots are excellent examples of **PORTABLE** items. They are smaller versions of computers that have been made into a size and weight easy to carry.

Thomas Jefferson **SUPPORTED** Lewis and Clark by providing funds for their exploration of the western part of the American continent. Meriweather Lewis and William Clark, and their team of explorers, had a difficult time on their travels when they had to **PORTAGE** (carry their canoes and all their supplies and equipment) over land between the rivers that **TRANSPORTED** them from their starting point in St. Louis, Missouri, to their western destination, the Pacific Ocean. On their return to Washington, D.C., they **REPORTED** to President Jefferson on all they had learned during their great historic journey.

**EXTRA WORDS:** A **REPORTER** is someone who goes out to find information or a news story and "carries back" (sometimes now by satellite link) the information for a specific audience. **COMPORTMENT** refers to behavior, or the way a person "carries" himself or herself. **Porta-potty**—a movable toilet, not connected to a sewer. ***Porte-monnaie***—the French word for wallet, or "carry money."

© 2003 J&J Lundquist

# novus

**[NOH woos]   new**

novel – (noun) a fictitious story of book length
novel – (adj.) of a new kind or nature, not previously known
novice – a beginner, an inexperienced person; a probationary member of a religious order, before taking of vows
novitiate – a novice or new person in a religious order
novelty – new in character and originality; a new or unusual occurrence; a small toy of novel design
*nouveau riche* (*French*) – newly rich
nova – a star that suddenly increases in brightness and then subsides
supernova – a star that suddenly increases in brightness and then explodes

**TEACHING NOTES:** **NOVEL**, when it refers to a book, comes from Latin through Italian from *"novella storia"*—new story. When **NOVEL** is an adjective, it describes something new. A **NOVICE** is someone without experience who is learning a new skill. In religion, someone who has entered a convent on a trial basis, with the intention of taking vows and joining an order, is called a **NOVITIATE**. Probably the most famous **NOVITIATE** is Maria in Rodgers and Hammerstein's ***The Sound of Music***.

A **NOVELTY** can mean something new or unusual, or it can refer to an object which is often useless, but, due to its new design, is either decorative or entertaining. *NOUVEAU RICHE* is a French term used to describe people who have recently become wealthy and are often a bit pretentious.

A **NOVA** was originally thought to be a new star, a star not previously recorded. Modern astronomy has determined that a **NOVA** is a star that suddenly increases in brightness (perhaps allowing our telescopes to see the star not visible at its normal brightness) and that gradually fades back to normal. A **SUPERNOVA** occurs when a star suddenly increases to a much greater brightness than a **NOVA**, and the intensity of the change causes the star to explode. The remnant (leftover material) of a supernova can either become a nebula, a neutron star, or a black hole. The most famous remnant of a **SUPERNOVA** in our Milky Way Galaxy is the Crab Nebula, left over from a star that exploded in 1054. This **SUPERNOVA** was so bright that it could be seen during the day for 23 days and, thereafter, for 653 nights. Chinese astronomers recorded seeing this **SUPERNOVA**; quite possibly the Anasazi people, too, who lived over 1,000 years ago in the area that later became Arizona and New Mexico. Can you find more **SUPERNOVAE**? (Romans changed -a to -ae to mean plural, or more than one.)

© 2003 J&J Lundquist

## ordo ordinis

**[OR do, OR din is]   row, array, command**

order – everything in its place; tidiness; a group, religious or other, living by the same rules; a command

orderly – systematically arranged, regular; obedient to rules

ordinary – regular, normal, customary, usual

ordinance – an authoritative order; a decree

ordinal number – number defining place in a series: first, second, etc.

extraordinary (extra L. - outside) – out of the ordinary; remarkable

*NOVUS ORDO SECLORUM* – "A New Order of the Ages" – motto on the Great Seal of the United States (on the back of a one dollar bill)

**TEACHING NOTES:** The word **ORDO** must have meant much to the ancient Romans because they were very **ORDERLY**. They were great engineers and builders of systems of all kinds. The city of Rome itself was an architectural wonder of its time. The system of Roman Law which they created for the lands they controlled made life in the Roman Empire relatively safe and reliable for its citizens. It is the basis for most systems of law in Western civilization today. The roads they built (all of which were said to lead to Rome!) were well-designed and constructed and served not only the Roman Army but a lively commerce which contributed to Rome's prosperity. Some of these roads still exist today! One can still stroll along the Appian Way, the most famous of all Roman roads!

The dictionary gives so many meanings for the word **ORDER** that we cannot include them all here, but looking them up is great fun! There are three **ORDERS** or styles in Greek architecture—Doric, Ionic, and Corinthian. Perhaps a student would like to find them in an encyclopedia and draw the capitals of some Doric, Ionic, and Corinthian columns for the class so everyone will be able to recognize them.

**EXTRA WORDS:** **INORDINATE** (in L. - not) – immoderate or excessive. **SUBORDINATE** (sub L. - under) – *noun*, one who takes orders from someone else; *adjective*, on a lower level; *verb,* to demote or place lower. **INSUBORDINATION** – defying or disregarding orders; acting above one's station or position; being "too big for one's boots."

© 2003 J&J Lundquist

# saeculum

### [SEYE koo loom]   age, century

secular – worldly as opposed to ecclesiastical or church-related
secularize – convert from church to civil property or use
*siècle* (*French*) – century (*fin de siècle* - end of the century)
NOVUS ORDO SECLORUM – "A New Order for the Ages"
secule – period of geologic time corresponding to strata in rocks

**TEACHING NOTES:** The Latin word **SAECULUM** (also spelled **SECULUM**) referred to an age or a long life span for a man—about a hundred years or so—a century. It also came to mean the world and its "wisdom of the ages" as opposed to religious teaching, and so the word **SECULAR** meant non-religious, the world of business, science, farming, and daily life. To **SECULARIZE** a piece of property meant to convert it from church uses to civil or private property.

The Great Seal of the United States, adopted in 1782, had on its reverse side, the words **NOVUS ORDO SECLORUM** which meant "a new order for the ages," intending to make clear that the new nation would not have a national religion. The government would be **SECULAR** and ensure freedom of worship for all who would come seeking religious freedom. The new arrangement of government was a great departure from the governments of monarchies with state religions from which the early American settlers had come. The Founding Fathers intended that a new plan for self-government for a free people should be created with the grand new design laid out in the Constitution of the United States. (Look for these words on the back of a dollar bill.)

In geology, a **SECULE** refers to the period of time which corresponds to a layer or stratum of rock, which helps geologists identify when fossils and other clues were laid down, allowing them to classify items according to the periods of geologic time.

**EXTRA WORDS:** *Fin de siècle* is a French phrase referring to the end of the 19th century—the 1890s—and describes art, music, and styles of dress or decor created in that period.

© 2003 J&J Lundquist

LATIN

# primus

**[PREE moos]  first**

primary – first in time or order of development; earliest; main
primer – first book of instruction in reading or other learning
prime – first in time, rank, degree, importance, quality
prime number – number that can be divided only by itself and 1
primate – order of mammals including humans, apes, monkeys, etc.
primitive – the conditions of life in earliest times before technology
primogeniture – custom of the eldest son in a family inheriting the family land and wealth
*prima donna* (*Italian* - first lady) – a leading lady of the opera

**TEACHING NOTES:**  PRIMUS is the first of what we call the ORDINAL numbers because they describe the order in which things come, as opposed to the CARDINAL numbers which we presented in Volume I. (See Vol. II, page 55 for **CARDO, CARDINIS**.) The distinction is not always easy for children to understand, but if they can remember that ORDINAL numbers tell the *order* of their place in line (first, second, third, etc.), while CARDINAL numbers are the numbers we see in a pack of *cards* (or use in counting items: one, two, three, etc.), perhaps it will be easier to remember.

The **PRIMARY** lessons in any school are the first or introductory lessons. Children begin their education in the **PRIMARY** grades. Early texts called **PRIMERS**, which featured carefully-selected vocabulary and simple sentence structure, were designed to be a student's first books to read. **PRIMERS** were to help students progress to all the subjects they would study in the future.

At the zoo, the **PRIMATE** house is where the monkeys, apes, lemurs, and tarsiers live. We often forget that in the broad categories of the animal kingdom, humans are also **PRIMATES**. We seldom refer to ourselves as **PRIMATES**, unless we are very high in rank or authority. When the word **Primate** is capitalized, it refers to the highest bishop in a province or nation.

The old custom of **PRIMOGENITURE**, which allowed the eldest son in a family to inherit the family's land and estates, caused the younger sons to leave home to "seek their fortunes." Sometimes younger sons would distinguish themselves through serving in the military, joining the clergy, going to sea to find new trade options, or following some other adventure. This system existed in many parts of the world, but not in the United States. In the United States, many of the great plantations in the South were founded by the younger sons of British noble families.

© 2003 J&J Lundquist

LATIN

# secundus

**[seh KOON doos]     second**

second – immediately following the first in order or rank; damaged or flawed new merchandise

second – an aide to a participant in a duel

second – a 60th of a minute

second hand – the hand marking seconds on a clock

secondhand – used clothing or equipment

secondary – next after first in time, priority, or order of development

secondary market – selling of stocks on the open market after an initial public offering of shares in a company

**TEACHING NOTES:**   In English we use the word **SECOND** in many ways that grow out of its basic meaning of "the next," or "following after the first." It acquired, even in Latin, the meaning of supporting or aiding. In the days when duels were fought, the antagonists brought along their "**SECONDS**" to help them see that the fight was conducted fairly and to care for the loser.

In meetings conducted in accordance with Robert's ***Rules of Order***, a motion that is made always requires a "**SECOND**" from someone who supports the motion before the issue can be debated. An introduction to Robert's ***Rules of Order*** would be a valuable exploration, as this widely-used method of conducting class or group business in a democracy is useful to everyone, even at an early age. A class which undertakes group projects can learn to conduct orderly meetings as early as first or second grade.

Stores sometimes advertise, at very reduced prices, **SECONDS** or merchandise which is new and usable but not of first quality due to flaws of some kind. Sometimes these goods are a bargain, and sometimes not! This kind of merchandise is not to be confused with **SECONDHAND** merchandise—items which have been owned and used but which can still be useful to someone. "Garage sales" are a good market for **SECONDHAND** goods, and they are popular everywhere.

Young children enjoy learning about stocks and bonds, saving the money they earn, and buying one or more shares of stock in companies they find interesting. They can learn how companies are formed, what determines their success or failure, and how they, as part owners, can share in the profits of the business. When entrepreneurs start new companies, they can raise capital by selling shares to whoever wants to buy them in an "initial public offering." These shares can then be sold to other buyers the next day in the **SECONDARY MARKET**.

© 2003 J&J Lundquist

LATIN

# tertius

**[TAIR tee oos]    third**

tertiary – third in order
tertiary color – color produced by mixing two secondary colors
tertiary period – the first period in the Cenozoic Era
Tertius/Tertia – names for a boy or girl who is the third child in a family
tertial (ornithology) – the third row of feathers in the wing of a bird
tertio-geniture – right of succession or inheritance belonging to the third born in a family
*tertius gaudens* (gaudere L. - to rejoice) – a third person who benefits from the conflict of two others

**TEACHING NOTES:** Every kindergarten child knows the primary colors: red, yellow, and blue. Most children recognize the secondary colors as well: orange, produced by mixing red and yellow; green, by mixing yellow and blue; and purple, produced by mixing blue with red. Beyond these are the **TERTIARY** colors: reddish orange, yellowish orange, yellowish green, bluish green, and so on. Advertising writers and fabric designers become quite poetic in describing these ever-more-complicated mixtures of color that the makers of clothing and paints use in manufacturing their merchandise. "Yellowish green" will not sell as many sweaters as "Chartreuse." Few "purplish blue" table or bed linens would appear in our homes, but "Periwinkle" and "Forget-me-not" linens invite us to bring our flower gardens indoors! Students may have a marvelous time mixing poster paints and then devising attractive names for their **TERTIARY** color formations. A good time will be had by all! Who knows? Like the great painter, Titian, whose trademark brownish red color is named after him, a student in the class may invent a new hue that will forever bear his or her name!

The **TERTIARY** period in geologic time was significant because it began just as the reptile dinosaurs became extinct 65 million years ago. Any good unabridged dictionary will give you a chart of geologic time which children will enjoy exploring. It will show that large mammals began to appear in the **TERTIARY** period of the Cenozoic Era (kainos G. - new, fresh + zoon G. - animal) after the dinosaurs died out, leaving the resources of the world to other kinds of animals.

© 2003 J&J Lundquist

# quartus

LATIN

### [KWAR toos]  fourth

quart – one-fourth of a gallon
quartile – one-fourth of the total group being tested in research
quarter – one-fourth of anything; one-fourth of the school year
quarter horse – strong, fast horse trained to race a quarter of a mile
quarto – paper folded twice to produce four sheets / eight pages
quarter-bound – book with leather on the spine, 1/4 of the cover
quarterdeck – the stern area of a sailing ship's upper deck
quarter note – musical note held for 1/4 of the time of a whole note
quarterly – recurring every three months; 1/4 of a year
quartet – four singers who sing in four-part harmony

**TEACHING NOTES:** While the cardinal number **QUATTUOR** (Vol. I, p. 36) gave us derivatives which meant four of something, the ordinal number **QUARTUS** means the fourth in order. It also means a fourth part of a whole, as the list above shows. A gallon of liquid is divided into four **QUARTS** or **QUARTER** parts. In statistical research, the whole group of people being tested or studied can be divided into four parts so that individual characteristics or test scores can be compared to those of the whole group. A fourth of the group will be in the top **QUARTILE**, and a fourth in each of the other three **QUARTILES**. The school year, usually coinciding with the seasons of the year, is divided into fall, winter, spring, and summer **QUARTERS**. Football games are divided into halves and **QUARTERS**.

In book publishing, large sheets of paper are printed and then folded before they are cut into a page size which determines the size of the finished book. In a **folio** size book, if the printed sheet is folded once, there are two leaves with four printed sides. If the sheet is folded twice, it will produce four leaves with eight printed sides in a **QUARTO** book. Students enjoy trying to produce books with a large sheet of folded newsprint to see how the pages must be printed so the book will have all the pages in numerical order and right side up! Books bound in beautiful, costly leather, are sometimes **QUARTER-BOUND** with the leather used only for the spine and a fourth of the cover.

On old sailing ships, the helmsman's raised afterdeck area, which covered about a fourth of the ship's deck, was called the **QUARTERDECK**. Beneath it was the captain's cabin. **QUARTER HORSES**, bred to be fast for racing a **QUARTER** of a mile, are also good horses for ranching jobs, like herding cows or catching rustlers.

© 2003 J&J Lundquist

LATIN

# quintus

**[KWEEN toos]    fifth**

quintile – in research statistics, one-fifth of the group being tested

quintessence – the essence of an idea in its most concentrated form

quintuplet – one-fifth of five offspring born at the same birth

quintuplicate – the fifth of five exact copies

quintet – group of five musicians or singers; music written for such a group

quinta (in Portugal, Spain, and Latin America) – a farm rented for one-fifth of the income it produces

**TEACHING NOTES:** The top **QUINTILE** in a group being studied or tested is the top fifth, or twenty percent of the whole group.

While multiple births are common among kittens and puppies, they are unusual among humans. When the Dionne **QUINTUPLETS** were born in Ontario, Canada, during the Depression of the 1930s, they were so rare and unusual that they were allowed by their parents (who could not afford to raise them) to be brought up in a kind of laboratory where they could be studied. Tourists were allowed to observe them at play and at work. They were not allowed to have normal childhoods and each **QUINTUPLET**, in later life, lamented the loss. Today, we hope their human rights would be better protected.

In government and in business, documents must be reproduced many times so each person concerned will have a copy. Computers have helped cut down on this paper blizzard somewhat, but some offices still provide **QUINTUPLICATE** paper copies of invoices, often in different colors, so that each person who has anything to do with an order gets a copy.

A **QUINTA** (pronounced "keén-ta") was originally a farm which a man could rent by paying the owner a fifth of the crop he was able to produce. In Spain, Portugal, and Latin America, a **QUINTA** has come to mean any country estate or villa outside a city. In the United States there is a motel chain called **LA QUINTA**, suggesting the comfort of this kind of rural retreat for travelers.

A **QUINTESSENCE** is the most purified and concentrated form of a non-material quality. Some people have tried to suggest "baseball, hot dogs, and apple pie" as the **QUINTESSENCE** of Americanism. Perhaps the students can think of other **QUINTESSENTIAL** symbols of such qualities as patriotism, scholarship, sportsmanship, fatherhood and motherhood, or nature in its most pristine form. How enlightening the resulting essays would be!

While we usually think of a **QUINTET** as a group of five singers or musicians, the **QUINTET** best known to many of us is a basketball team! If they can play in harmony, all the better!

© 2003 J&J Lundquist

LATIN

# sextus

**[SEX toos]   sixth**

sext – sixth canonical hour of the day; noon
siesta (*Spanish* from L. sexta hora - noon) – an afternoon nap or rest
sextant – a navigational tool with an arc which is 1/6 of a circle
sextuplet – one of six babies born at one birth
sextet – a group of six musicians
sestet – a six-line poem, or the last six lines of an Italian sonnet
sexagesimal – one-sixtieth of anything

**TEACHING NOTES:** There are very few human births which produce **SEXTUPLETS**. When it happens, it is big news and a cause for headlines all over the world. After caring for so many babies at once, parents would most likely be in need of a **SIESTA** on a daily basis, as is the custom in many Spanish-speaking countries.

A **SEXTANT** is a navigational instrument invented in both England and America in 1731. It is used for measuring the altitude of celestial objects (such as the sun, moon, or stars) in relation to an imaginary plane which extends out from a ship on the ocean to the horizon. To measure this angle, a **SEXTANT** has a graduated arc (labeled with degrees) which is *one-sixth* of a circle (60°). By figuring out the angle to the heavenly body at a specific time of day, and then consulting the *Nautical Almanac*, the navigator can then calculate the ship's position at sea. GPS (Global Positioning System) devices have taken most of this kind of calculation out of determining positions at sea, but in the event of equipment failure, boaters still need to understand celestial navigation. A **SEXTANT** is also used by land surveyors in measuring and mapping tracts of land. Perhaps someone could bring a **SEXTANT** to class, or at least a picture of one.

An Italian sonnet is a fourteen-line poem which begins with an *octave*, or eight lines, featuring a specific rhyme scheme, followed by a **SESTET** of six lines with a different rhyme scheme. The Italian sonnet is a form of poetry favored by such great poets as John Milton, Elizabeth Barrett Browning, and William Wordsworth. Two possible rhyme schemes for an Italian sonnet are: *abbaabba cdcdcd* or *abbaabba cdecde*. It would be interesting to put a sonnet on an overhead projector so the class could discover the rhyme scheme together. Someone in class could research how an Italian sonnet differs from an English or Shakespearean sonnet. Read some good examples of sonnets, and then everyone in class can have a go at writing his or her own!

© 2003 J&J Lundquist

LATIN

# septimus

### [SEP ti moos]   seventh

**septimal** – seventh; of the number seven
**septime** – the seventh of the eight parrying positions in fencing
**septuplet** – one of seven babies born at one birth
**Septuagesima Sunday** – the seventieth day before Easter; third Sunday before Lent
**September** – seventh month of the old Roman calendar

**TEACHING NOTES:** **SEPTIMUS, -A, -UM**: These ordinal numbers are adjectives, because they describe nouns. The Latin forms have different endings: -us (masculine); -a (feminine); and -um (neuter), depending on the gender of the noun they modify. Our nouns in English don't have to be considered male or female, except when gender is obvious (boy, girl, man, woman), so we don't attach endings which make practically everything masculine or feminine. Sailors usually refer to their ships as "she," and we're sure they have their own reasons for doing so; but books, bottles, and bandwagons, like most nouns in English, are happily free of gender. In Latin dictionaries, however, you will rarely find a noun that isn't followed by "m." for masculine or "f." for feminine. Neuter nouns in Latin are few and far between.

**QUINTUS, SEXTUS, SEPTIMUS,** and **OCTAVIUS** were names sometimes given to children in Roman families. Perhaps this was to avoid confusion over inheritance in a society where the practice of primogeniture conveyed the bulk of the family estate to the eldest son. In the British Empire, following the example of the Romans, families took up the practice of using number adjectives as names for their children. Two brothers of the English poet, Elizabeth Barrett Browning, were named **SEPTIMUS** and **OCTAVIUS**.

The term **SEPTIME** is used primarily in fencing and sword play. There are eight parts of the upper torso of the swordsman where he can be fairly hit, and so there are eight defending or parrying positions of his foil or sword to protect those areas and ward off a touch or hit. Fencing is an Olympic sport, and it is helpful to learn these terms to better understand and appreciate the skill and artistry of good fencing competition. An Internet search for "fencing clubs" will give a wealth of information. The parrying positions have French names which are French versions of the Latin ordinal numbers: right shoulder # 3 **TIERCE**; left shoulder # 1 **PRIME**; right chest # 6 **SIXTE**; left chest # 4 **QUARTE**; upper abdomen right # 2 **SECONDE**; upper abdomen left # 5 **QUINTE**; waist abdomen right # 8 **OCTAVE**; waist abdomen left # 7 **SEPTIME**. These positions don't seem to be logically placed, so drawing a diagram will help to visualize them.

© 2003 J&J Lundquist

# octavus

**[ohk TAH woos]   eighth**

Octavius – family name of Augustus Caesar
octave – series of eight notes in music
octavo – a size of book or printed page (about 6 × 9 inches)
October – eighth month of the old Roman calendar

**TEACHING NOTES:** Augustus Caesar, first Emperor of Rome, was born Gaius **OCTAVIUS** (or *Octavian*) and named after his father, Senator Gaius **OCTAVIUS**. The senator died when his son was only four years old. **OCTAVIUS** was his family name, so *Octavian* was not given the name on account of his being the eighth child in his family. His grandmother was Julia, the sister of Julius Caesar. Caesar had no sons and adopted little **OCTAVIUS** in his will. However, **OCTAVIUS** only learned about this when Julius Caesar was assassinated. He was serving Caesar as a military officer in Illyria (now Albania) when he heard the news. He went directly to Rome (at the age of 18) and began gathering support for his own elevation to the rank of emperor. The story of how he became the best of the long line of Rome's emperors is fascinating and would be a great research project! He was responsible for much of the greatness of the Roman Empire and for the value placed on Roman citizenship.

In the early days of printing, books were printed on large sheets of paper and then folded and cut to form the book pages (see **QUARTO**, page 64). When a large sheet of paper was folded three times, it produced 8 leaves or 16 printed pages for a book size called **OCTAVO** (try this with a large sheet of newsprint paper). This set of eight leaves, called a "signature," was cut on three sides with the last folded side left uncut so the signature could be sewn together or bound with other signatures into the full-length book called an **OCTAVO**. A smaller book called a **duodecimo** (12) was made by folding the large sheet into 12 leaves or 24 pages. Book sizes vary according to who publishes them, but most hardback trade books are **OCTAVOS**. Many paperbacks are **duodecimos**. Large "coffee table books" may be **QUARTOS** or even **folios**.

The **OCTAVE** in music is supposed to be eight notes (*Do, Re, Mi, Fa, Sol, La, Ti, Do*). Some musicians think it should be called a **SEPTIME**, because the eighth note is another *Do* and part of the next **SEPTIME**. Most people, however, consider *Do* to *Do* an octave so it most likely won't change!

© 2003 J&J Lundquist

LATIN

# nonus

### [NO noos]  ninth

nonagenarian – a person aged 90-99
nones – (Christian Church) the ninth hour after *prime* or sunrise; the devotional service performed then
nonet – a group of nine singers or musicians
nonagon – a polygon having 9 angles and 9 sides
noon – (from nones) 12:00; midday

**TEACHING NOTES:** The derivatives from this Latin word for ninth are few, partly because the number nine has less relation to the rhythms of nature in our daily lives (except on a baseball diamond) than any of the other numbers. We have ten fingers, five on each hand; seven days in a week; four seasons and four cardinal directions; etc.

The word **NONE** is spelled the same as the word *none*, meaning not one. **NONE** is used primarily as a church term for one of the specific times of day (3:00 p.m.) when prayers are to be offered in a convent or monastery. Known as canonical hours (according to ecclesiastical edict or canon law) and beginning with *matins* (12 midnight), prayers were scheduled for *lauds* (3:00 a.m.), *prime* (6:00 a.m.), *tierce* (9:00 a.m.), *sext* (12 noon), **NONES** (3:00 p.m.), *vespers* (6:00 p.m.), and *compline* (9:00 p.m.). These hours followed the Roman tradition of only numbering the daylight hours, therefore, *prime* was the first hour of daylight, *tierce* was the third hour after sunrise, etc.

How did our word **NOON**, come to mean 12:00 midday instead of 3:00 p.m.? There were probably several factors influencing this change, including the unreliability of timekeeping devices in use during the Middle Ages. The extended hours of daylight during summer months may have skewed the actual hours at which services were performed as the sun rose earlier and set later. During religious holidays requiring fasting, people were allowed to break their fast after the church service offered at **NONES** (3:00 p.m.). In some Benedictine monasteries, the service for **NONES** came to be performed any time after **SEXT**, thereby relaxing the hour of the **NONES** or *NOON* meal. While the general public was not required to observe the overnight services, monks were expected to rise and pray at the hours of *matins* and *lauds*. The French immortalized the concern monks had with oversleeping in the familiar children's song, *Frère Jacques, Frère Jacques, Dormez vous? Dormez vous? Sonnez les matines, Sonnez les matines. Din Don Din, Din Don Din.*

The need to pray on time inspired the earliest technology of timekeeping such as water clocks and, later, mechanical clocks, watches, chronometers, etc. (See: *Revolution in Time; Clocks and the Making of the Modern World* by D. S. Landes. New York: Barnes and Noble Books, 1983, Section I, Finding Time) (www.uh.edu/engines/epi1376.htm).

© 2003 J&J Lundquist

LATIN

# decimus

**[DEH ki moos]   tenth**

decimate – destroy a tenth part of
decimal system – base ten number system
Dewey Decimal System – system for classifying library books
decimeter – one-tenth of a meter; 3.94 inches
deciliter – one-tenth of a liter; 0.21 pint
decigram – one-tenth of a gram; 1.543 grains
decimalization – conversion to a decimal system (as of a currency)
dime – 10-cent coin; one-tenth of a dollar

**TEACHING NOTES:** The system of weights and measures in American society is a curious mixture. The numeral system we use is the **Decimal System**, sometimes called base 10, and our monetary currency has been **DECIMALIZED**, with a **DIME** being one-tenth of a dollar bill. When the country was still in its colonial period, we used the British monetary system of pounds sterling, with the pound divided into crowns (4 per pound), shillings (20 per pound), sixpence (2 per shilling), pence (12 per shilling), farthings (4 per penny). A sovereign was a one-pound coin, and a guinea was one pound and a shilling. We also used Spanish dollars, doubloons, and pieces of eight. In 1792, Congress passed the Coinage Act, making the American dollar the basic unit of United States currency and creating a **DECIMAL** system which was easier to use. Coins were minted for circulation with half dollars, quarters, **DIMES**, nickels, and pennies as fractional units of the dollar. In 1971, the British adopted the New Penny, which was equal to one-hundredth of a pound. This **DECIMALIZED** system made money calculations easier in England.

Early libraries had various systems for classifying their collections, our favorite being the one where "neatness counts." They put all the folio size books together, all the quartos, all the octavos, all the duodecimos, etc. The shelves looked tidy, and no doubt this worked for a fairly small collection. However, in 1876, Melvil Dewey devised the **DEWEY DECIMAL SYSTEM**, using the Arabic number system from 000 – 999. One thousand *"sections"* identified broad categories of subjects which were then subdivided by adding a decimal point and more numbers to narrow down specialized information about each subject. For example: **590** Zoological Sciences; **594** Mollusca; **595** Other invertebrates; **599** Mammals. Learning this system early makes using the library quick, easy, and very satisfying. Find INSECTS among the invertebrates in **595.7**! With the card catalog, you can be your own librarian!

© 2003 J&J Lundquist

GREEK

ελεκτρον

# elektron

**[eh LEK tron]   amber**

**electricity** – a fundamental natural entity of negative and positive kinds; observable in attraction or repulsion of bodies and in natural phenomena such as lightning or aurora borealis
**electric** – relating to or operated by electricity
**electron** – elementary particle consisting of a negative charge of electricity
**electrician** – one who installs, maintains, and repairs electrical equipment

**TEACHING NOTES:** Connecting **amber** with **ELECTRICITY** requires an interesting historical explanation. **Amber** has long been valued not only for its beauty but also for its almost magical ability to attract small objects like feathers or straw after being rubbed with a cloth. The Greek philosopher Thales of Miletus, a Greek colony on the coast of Asia Minor—now Turkey, was the first person known to observe these properties in **amber** back in the 6th century B.C. This early discovery of what we now know as static **ELECTRICITY** led to constant inquiry and experiment throughout history. **Amber**, called *elektron* by the Greeks, had been brought to Greece by travelers from the Baltic Sea, where they found it on the coasts of present-day Poland and Lithuania. It had begun to form 50 million years ago as sticky tree resin which oozed down the tree trunks, collecting any bugs or other debris in its path. It then hardened into the jewel-like translucent substance **amber** that we value so highly today. The fanciful idea that some of this resin oozed out of a tree more than sixty-five million years ago, while dinosaurs still lived, and that a mosquito, having drunk dinosaur blood, was then caught in the sticky resin and turned into **amber**, was dramatized in the book and movie *Jurassic Park*. The author, Michael Crichton, imagined that modern scientists were able to extract the dinosaur's DNA from the blood in the stomach of the mosquito in the **amber** and then to recreate or clone the extinct dinosaurs.

William Gilbert, an English physician in 1600, compared the attraction of **amber** (he called it *electrum*), which attracted very light things like feathers, to the magnetic properties of lodestones, which were attracted to anything made of iron. He found other substances which behaved like amber and called them all **electrica**. These discoveries helped set the stage for Benjamin Franklin, who was interested in **ELECTRICITY** and did a famous experiment with a kite and a key in a storm, showing that lightning is **ELECTRICITY**. Today we can hardly imagine our world without the energy provided for all that we do by **ELECTRICITY**. Students may enjoy tracing the history of the development of **ELECTRICAL** power.

© 2003 J&J Lundquist

LATIN

# gradus

### [GRAH doos]   step, degree

grade – a degree or step in a scale of rank, quality, value
gradual – taking place, changing, or moving in small degrees
graduation – ceremony of giving diplomas or degrees in school or college for completion of a program
gradient – rate of regular or graded ascent or descent; inclination
centigrade (centum L. - hundred) – a scale of measuring heat which has one hundred degrees between water's freezing and boiling points; Celsius' thermometer
egress (e, ex L. - go out) – a way out of an enclosed space; an exit
regress (re L. - again, back) – a step back to a former position

**TEACHING NOTES:** Civilization, from the days of early man, has progressed one step at a time. The Latin word **GRADUS**, meaning step or degree, has given us many derivatives. **GRADUAL** changes are not as upsetting as are radical shifts in our daily lives. Yet, when we look at the changes we have seen in 100 years, we are shocked at the vast differences in people's lives! It's interesting for children to think and write about what has happened in the last century in our cities, our countryside, our houses, in how we travel, and in how we communicate. But the changes happened **GRADUALLY**, just as children grow—so **GRADUALLY** that the changes seem imperceptible. Aesop's fable of the race between the hare and the tortoise has helped thousands of children realize that, step by step, slow and steady wins the race. Children are often amazed to hear that college level work will not be any harder for them than their lessons in **GRADE** school, provided they master each step in their learning along the way.

With the help of paths or roads constructed with an easy **GRADIENT**, we can walk right up the highest mountains! One reason history is so fascinating is that we can look back with a bird's eye view on events which took years to unfold or develop and see the steps that were taken and their consequences. This leads to the happy state of perspective. Encourage children to keep journals of the small happenings in their lives. These records will gain in value every year as they continue to write in them.

While the United States uses the Fahrenheit scale for temperature, the **CENTIGRADE** scale is used in most other places around the world, and children should be familiar with the differences. Have children figure out how to dress for a day where the forecast is for 33° Fahrenheit, and then for 33° Celsius. Knowing which scale is being used could be the difference between choosing to wear a down parka or shorts!

© 2003 J&J Lundquist

# plus
# pluris

**[PLOOS, PLOO ris]   more, many**

plus – more, additional
plus sign – in mathematics, (+) meaning additional or positive value
plural – more than one in number
plurality – a larger or greater number, though not an absolute majority
*E PLURIBUS UNUM* – "out of many (states), one (nation)"
surplus (super L. - above) – extra, more or above what is needed
nonplussed – "not more" – perplexed; not knowing what more to say
plus fours – men's long baggy knickers worn for golfing in the 1920s

**TEACHING NOTES:** This Latin word **PLUS** has come into English just "as is." It is a comparative adjective and is declined to make it agree with the noun it modifies. Look at the discussion of Latin declensions on page 11, where the word OMNIBUS is explained. We have that "-IBUS" ending again in **PLURIBUS** because of the preposition **E** which comes before it. The Latin dictionary will tell you that **EX** or **E**, meaning "out of," must take the ablative case. **EX** is used before words beginning with a vowel, and **e** before words beginning with a consonant. The Founding Fathers knew their Latin when they placed the motto, "Out of many (states), one (nation)" **E PLURIBUS UNUM**, on coins and dollar bills.

While Tiger Woods, the icon of the golf world, draws attention wherever he goes, the late Payne Stewart made a stir by bucking modern golfing fashions and wearing **PLUS FOURS**, the old-fashioned trousers gathered below the knee and favored by golfers in the early decades of the 20th century. **PLUS FOURS** were named for the four extra inches of material that extended below the knee and bloused over, allowing for freedom of movement.

The **PLUS SIGN** indicates a positive value to be added to find a sum in mathematics. When using an Internet search engine, the **PLUS SIGN** can be used instead of the word "and" to narrow the results. Using Boolean Logic, a search engine sorts through countless Websites according to the indicators the user specifies: *AND* (+), *OR*, or *NOT* (-). For instance, if you would like to find information on the ceiling of the Sistine Chapel painted by Michelangelo, your search might be: Michelangelo + Sistine Chapel. This will restrict the search to only those Websites which mention *both* Michelangelo *AND* the Sistine Chapel, and weed out any of the sites which mention *either* Michelangelo *OR* the Sistine Chapel but not both in the same site. Since Michelangelo was primarily a sculptor, a request for (Michelangelo+Sistine Chapel+ceiling) -sculpture, would eliminate many more sites. Knowing how to narrow the range of searches will become increasingly important as the number of Web sites continues to expand.

© 2003 J&J Lundquist

**GREEK**

ακρος

# akros

**[AH kross]    topmost; high point; extreme**

acrobat (bainein G. - to go) – one who performs gymnastic feats on a high wire, elevated apparatus, or on the ground

acrobatics – art of an acrobat; aviation stunts high in the air

acropolis (polis G. - city, Vol. I, p. 83) – high point of a Greek city; a citadel

Acropolis – the hill in Athens on which the Parthenon, the Temple of Athena, was built

acronym (onyma G. - name) – word formed from the first letters of a phrase: radar, scuba, NATO, NAFTA, etc.

acrophobia – extreme fear of heights

**TEACHING NOTES:** ACROBATS have always inspired awe and admiration for their physical feats of daring. While old circuses relied on trained animals to draw crowds and perhaps featured an ACROBAT as a diversion between animal acts, the now famous *Cirque du Soleil* has left the animals at home and focused on ACROBATICS as the main draw for its audience. ACROBATS must be at the height of physical condition as they perform feats requiring great strength and flexibility, sometimes high above a stage without a net below. This would *not* be a job for a person with ACROPHOBIA! Pilots who execute loops and rolls with their airplanes are performing aerial ACROBATICS, a favorite at air shows.

The Greeks chose the highest hill in a city as the site to build a temple, so that the city's most important building could be defended. The highest point was called an ACROPOLIS. *The* ACROPOLIS (capitalized) in Athens is the most famous hill in Greece and the site of the Parthenon, the Temple of Athena, Goddess of Wisdom and the patron goddess of the city. Centuries of exposure to the elements took their toll on the famous temple. The Parthenon, used as an ammunition dump under the Turkish rule of Greece, blew up in 1687, destroying the entire center portion of the structure. The remaining fragments of the frieze from the pediment of the Parthenon and many of the damaged sculptures were salvaged by Lord Elgin, the British ambassador to the Turkish court. The "Elgin Marbles" are now carefully preserved and on display in The British Museum in London.

An ACRONYM takes the first letter(s) of each word in a phrase and makes a word that can be pronounced on its own. Scuba divers use a **S**elf **C**ontained **U**nderwater **B**reathing **A**pparatus. At airports, air traffic controllers use **RA**dio **D**etection **a**nd **R**anging, or radar, to locate incoming planes. Students can turn their own names into ACRONYMS by using a character trait or quality they admire and would like to exhibit for each letter in their name. Having students write down *good* qualities they notice in classmates can help them form the habit of looking for the good in others and in realizing how their own behavior affects others.

© 2003 J&J Lundquist

GREEK

κατα

# kata

### [KAH tah]   down, against

catalog (legein G. - to pick, choose) – a list from which to choose
catastrophe (strophein G. - to turn) – downturn of events
catapult (pallein G. - to hurl) – a device for hurling stones or arrows
cataract (rassein G. - to strike, smite) – a waterfall or downpouring of water; abnormality of the eye; clouded lens
catalyst (lysis G. - break, loose, set free) – person or thing that causes an event or change in the status quo
cataclysm (klyzein G. - to wash or dash over) – violent upheaval especially of a social or political nature; sudden action producing change in the earth's surface
catacomb (cumba G. - tomb) – subterranean cemetery

**TEACHING NOTES:** The **CATACOMBS** were underground burial chambers and tunnels carved out of rock in and around Rome. Because Christians were persecuted in ancient Rome, they found they could escape unwanted attention if they held religious services in the **CATACOMBS**, where no one else wanted to go. The **CATACOMBS** also provided a pleasant escape from the blistering heat in Rome.

While **CATALOG** originally meant any generic list, the word has evolved to mean a systematically arranged list, including particulars on the items included (price, color, etc.). Universities issue course **CATALOGS** listing all the classes available to students, and archeologists digging in ancient sites carefully **CATALOG** each artifact discovered and its original location. Each student should get acquainted with the local public library's card **CATALOG** system (see p. 70 on the Dewey Decimal System).

A **CATASTROPHE** can be either a natural phenomenon like an earthquake, hurricane, or blizzard, which is a sudden downturn of events interrupting the smooth progress of people's lives (known in the insurance world as "an act of God"), or it can be a reversal of fortune in a war or a military campaign like Napoleon's retreat from Moscow in the winter of 1812. Although Napoleon's **CATASTROPHE** was seen as "divine deliverance" by the Russians, it was seen by the French government more as the result of poor planning by Napoleon than as supernatural intervention. Either way, it was a definite "downer."

The Romans constructed **CATAPULTS** outside the walls of cities to loft heavy stones and other missiles to destroy the walls of cities they were besieging. They could then rain arrows down on the hapless inhabitants. The **CATAPULT** was a kind of huge, wooden slingshot which helped the Romans win many victories and extend their empire. These war machines were used well into medieval times. Modern, high-tech **CATAPULTS** launch Navy pilots in their planes from the deck of aircraft carriers, since the runway is too short to accommodate take-offs without a little extra oomph.

© 2003 J&J Lundquist

76

GREEK

αva

# ana

### [AH nah]   up, back again, along, through

analysis (luein G. - loosen, undo) – taking something apart to study it

anadromous (dromein G. - to run) – to run up, as fish swimming upstream from salt water to fresh water to spawn

anatomy (tome G. - cut, incision) – cutting up a body to study it; dissection

anachronism (chronos G. - time) – person or thing that belongs to another time; error in chronology

anagram (gram G. - written) – word, phrase, or sentence formed from another by rearranging its letters

analog (logos G. - word, Vol. I, p. 15) – displaying a readout by a pointer on a dial rather than numerical digits

analogy – similarity of two things such as a heart and a pump

**TEACHING NOTES:** The process of **ANALYSIS** is one of breaking up anything into smaller parts in order to study and better understand it, whether a machine, a biological or botanical specimen, or a thought process or an argument. The Greeks, early developers of western scientific inquiry, were always asking questions. Finding answers bit by bit allowed them to arrive at some astonishingly accurate conclusions, such as finding the circumference of the earth to within a few hundred feet.

When historical drama, whatever the medium (theatre, film, or television) is being produced, it is important to see that all details of scenery and costumes are historically correct and that **ANACHRONISMS** are not overlooked. For example, an actor playing a Roman soldier must remove his wrist watch, and a lady in a Civil War drama could not wear blue jeans. A statesman at the time of the American Revolution must not exclaim "Holy Guacamole!" and he would not jingle any car keys!

Students enjoy the **ANAGRAM** game of seeing how many words they can find in the letters of a word like **ANADROMOUS**. (Examples: drama, sad, mad, ran, run, sun, drum, door, etc. See others?)

The study of **ANATOMY** has been controversial (and sacrilegious to some) all through history, because dissection was needed to learn about the internal structures of the body. However, knowledge of the placement and function of internal organs and muscles has led to countless medical cures. Michelangelo gained knowledge of **ANATOMY** in secret dissection sessions, which also helped him create remarkably realistic portrayals of the body. His statue of David and the human figures in the Sistine Chapel show that his understanding of the operation of muscles was superior to that of previous artists.

© 2003 J&J Lundquist

LATIN

# duco
# ductum

**[DOO ko, DOOK toom]     draw, attract, lead**

**aqueduct** (<u>aqua</u> L. - water) – tube or canal for water to move along
**conduct** (<u>con</u> L. - together) – guide, direct, lead, convey
**deduct** (<u>de</u> L. - down from, away) – lead away, remove, subtract
**induct** (<u>in</u> L. - in, into) – lead or bring into
**produce** (<u>pro</u> L. - for, forward) – bring forth, make, cause, create
**surplus** (<u>super</u> L. - above) – extra, more or above what is needed
**viaduct** (<u>via</u> L. - way) – bridge over a valley for a road or train track; crossroad under a bridge or other obstruction
**reduce** (<u>re</u> L. - back) – to lead back; to bring down to a smaller size, amount, weight, or price

**TEACHING NOTES:** The great Roman engineers built elaborate **AQUEDUCT** systems designed to **CONDUCT** fresh, cool water from mountain streams to the hot, crowded city of Rome and other cities in the empire for use in drinking and cooking. The Tiber River ran through the city of Rome, so water was close by, but it was polluted with a brown silt that made it undesirable for drinking. The **AQUEDUCTS** brought into the city clean water that the citizens could access at various points around town. Some of Rome's famous fountains (built much later) are still fed by these ancient aqueducts.

In a good unabridged dictionary, you can find dozens of other derivatives when you look up each of the words in the list in our derivative box.

Ask students to imagine how a **DEDUCTION** taken on an income tax return could come from the same Latin root as **DEDUCTIVE** reasoning in logic. What does an old Roman **AQUEDUCT** have in common with **DUCT** tape, which is so widely used today to seal and repair the ducts which transport heat from the furnace to rooms in a house? How could a symphony **CONDUCTOR** share the same root as an award for good **CONDUCT**?

To **REDUCE** means to scale back to a lower level—whether it is a person's weight, the price of sale items in a store, the number of soldiers deployed in a war (a **REDUCTION** in force), or the amount of money available to be spent in a national (or household) budget. Such **REDUCTIONS** usually require leadership and good management so as to keep an enterprise able to accomplish its objectives and still maintain a healthy equilibrium.

© 2003 J&J Lundquist

LATIN

# ago actum

**[AH go, AHK toom]   do, act, drive, perform**

act – do, perform, behave
agent – a person or thing that causes an action to take place
agile – able to act quickly physically or mentally; nimble
ambiguous (ambi L. - both) – lead in two directions; unclear
navigate (navis L. - boat) – drive or steer a boat
coagulate (con L. - together) – drive liquid molecules together; clot, curdle, congeal, jell
prodigal (pro L. - forth) – driving forth, wasteful, extravagant

**TEACHING NOTES:** This little three letter word, **AGO**, is a gold mine of English derivatives! We couldn't list them all above, but you can expand your own vocabulary by adding prefixes and suffixes to the various derivatives you will find. Look for the words in the derivative list above in the biggest dictionary you can find and see what other forms of the words are listed nearby. In a Latin dictionary, verbs are listed with the four principal parts like this: AGO, AGERE, EGI, ACTUM. We give you the **first** and **fourth** principal parts to learn since the spelling is often quite different and, without knowing both, you might not recognize some of the derivatives as coming from the root word with the same meaning or idea.

As you can see, some of the derivatives come from the first principal part **AGO**. It's easy to see it in **AGENT** and **COAGULATE** because of the AG. **NAVIGATE** and **PRODIGAL** are less obvious because the *a* has changed to *i* for ease of pronunciation, but you still have the *g* to guide you.

The fourth principal part, **ACTUM**, exchanges the *g* for *c* because it is easier to pronounce a *c* than a *g* before *t*. (Try it and see for yourself.)

**AGENT** (a doer or **ACTOR** – sometimes on behalf of an **ACTOR**) gives you **AGENCY** and **AGENDA**.
**NAVIGATE** (steer a boat) yields **NAVIGATION, NAVIGABLE, UNNAVIGABLE, NAVIGATOR**.
**COAGULATE** (clot or jell) gives you **COAGULATION, COAGULABILITY, COAGULUM**.
**PRODIGAL** (wasteful) expands your word list with **PRODIGALITY, PRODIGALLY, PRODIGALIZE**.
**ACT** (do, perform) gives you **ACTION, ACTIVE, ACTIVITY, ACTOR, ACTRESS, ACTUAL, ENACT, EXACT, REACT, COUNTERACT, TRANSACT, RETROACTIVE**, and others.

Students would benefit from finding the definitions of these words and writing them in a notebook. Practice of this kind makes using a dictionary an easy and satisfying lifelong habit.

© 2003 J&J Lundquist

LATIN

# pendo
# pensum

### [PEN do, PAIN sum]
### hang down, weigh, consider, judge

pensive – weighing things in one's mind; thoughtful; reflective

suspend (sub L. - under) – to hang down under; temporarily stop an act

suspense – state of mental uncertainty while awaiting a decision or outcome

suspenders – adjustable shoulder straps with ends attached to the waistband of a pair of trousers

suspension – hanging down under something above; liquid throughout which particles are evenly distributed and do not settle to the bottom

expensive (e, ex L. - out) – entailing great expense; much weighing out

expend – to weigh out; to pay out; to use up (as energy or resources)

**TEACHING NOTES:** People have always needed to compare weights of animals, grain, money, etc. They invented a balance scale on which two pans were **SUSPENDED**, one from each end of a balanced horizontal bar. They then put something of known weight on one pan and the unknown on the other pan. It would be fun to make a balance scale out of a wire hanger and two jar lids suspended under each end to show this concept. You can put a known weight on one lid—perhaps a quarter pound of butter—and then balance it with coins, small pebbles, nuts, etc. The classic statue of JUSTICE shows a blindfolded (and therefore impartial) woman holding a balance scale on which she has hung the arguments of each side in a lawsuit. She will give her fair and balanced judgment to the side with the weightiest arguments.

    **SUSPENSE** is a favorite storytelling device an author uses to keep readers turning the pages until the very end when they will discover the solution to the mystery or how the hero and/or heroine manage(s) to survive the difficulties facing them. **SUSPENSE** is felt by anyone awaiting an outcome such as a grade on a test.

    A **SUSPENSION** bridge is one having two or more upright posts at intervals across the expanse to be bridged. Cables are anchored solidly at either end of the span and then **SUSPENDED** from the posts. The bridge deck, which people walk or drive across, is **SUSPENDED** from the cable. A picture of the Golden Gate Bridge in San Francisco will illustrate this engineering marvel. **SUSPENSION** also means to stop an activity temporarily (leave it hanging) while some correction is made, such as removal from work or school for disciplinary purposes.

    In the early days of buying and selling, when the butcher, the baker, and the candlestick maker traded among themselves, the buyer had to weigh out—**EXPEND**—enough grain (or bread) to equal the value of the shoes, meat, or candlesticks he wanted to buy from the seller. This kind of trading was called barter. Bartering faded out after money became widely used as a medium of exchange, but it is still used today in many parts of the world and in the backyard trading in the United States. Most people prefer to use money since the value of each coin or dollar bill is known, but they still weigh in their own minds whether the price charged by a seller is too **EXPENSIVE**, or a fair exchange and a good bargain.

© 2003 J&J Lundquist

GREEK

ὑπερ

# hyper

### [HOO pair, HEYE purr] above, overly, beyond

hyperbole (ballein G. - throw) – throw beyond; exaggerate
hyperactive (ago G. - do, act) – displaying excessive physical energy
hypercritical – overly critical; carping
hyperextension (ex L. - out, tendere L. - stretch) – extension of a body part beyond normal limits
hyperglycemia (glykys G. - sweet, haima G. - blood) – abnormally high level of glucose in the blood
hyperventilate (ventus L. - wind) – to breathe extremely fast and deeply
hypertrophy (trophe G. - nutrition) – excessive growth or development of a body part from over-nutrition or overuse

**TEACHING NOTES:** This word **HYPER** has an almost unlimited collection of derivatives. It is used frequently as an English word by itself. "Don't be so **HYPER**!" means "Don't overdo it!" Because it is quite generally understood, it is tacked on to many other English words. We have chosen a few of these "hybrid" derivatives in the list above: **HYPERACTIVE** and **HYPERCRITICAL**.

The medical profession makes "hyper-use" of **HYPER** to describe dozens of conditions which are caused by an excess of almost anything. Sports injuries often are caused by the **HYPEREXTENSION** of joints, knees, elbows, or fingers, resulting in pain or tearing which then must be repaired or treated. Some people who are shocked, surprised, or over-excited about something may start to **HYPERVENTILATE**, meaning that they are breathing too fast and too deeply. **HYPERVENTILATING** causes a rapid increase in oxygen and a decrease in carbon dioxide in the blood which can result in dizziness or can cause someone to faint.

Body-builders are sometimes said to have **HYPERTROPHY**, or over-development of the muscles, causing them to be musclebound or inflexible due to too much muscle mass. Hypertrophy is the opposite of *atrophy*, or the loss of muscle tone.

The term **HYPERGLYCEMIA** refers to an abnormally high level of glucose (sugar) in the blood, which must be corrected by various treatments. Diabetics contend with this problem constantly. Glucose in the blood is controlled by the production of insulin in the body. Insulin helps convert the glucose to energy to be burned up. In some diabetics, the body does not produce enough insulin to manage blood sugar, so they must supplement their own insulin production with insulin shots. Constantly monitoring blood sugar levels is important for diabetics since injections of insulin, vigorous exercise, or long intervals between meals can cause *hypoglycemia* (or abnormally *low* blood sugar, see *hypo*, p. 81). Non-diabetics can become **hypoglycemic**. Untreated, both *HYPER-* and *HYPOGLYCEMIA* can become life-threatening.

© 2003 J&J Lundquist

GREEK

ʽυπο

# hypo

**[HOO poh, HEYE poh]    under, below**

hypodermic (<u>dermis</u> L. - skin) – under the skin

hypochondria (<u>chondros</u> G. - cartilage of the breastbone) – excessive worry about one's health

hypothermia (<u>thermos</u> - heat) – having a body temperature below normal

hypocritical (<u>krinein</u> G. - distinguish, separate) – pretending to hold publicly approved values, but not practicing them

hypothesis (<u>thesis</u> G. - put, place) (hi-POTH-i-sis) – a proposition assumed for the sake of argument

hypoallergenic (<u>allos</u> G. - other; <u>genos</u> G. - kind) – designed to prevent an allergic response by containing few irritating substances

**TEACHING NOTES:**   A **HYPODERMIC** needle is widely used in medicine to go under the skin to extract blood samples or to inject medications or inoculations.

A **HYPOCHONDRIAC** is constantly worried that there is something wrong with his or her health. He is melancholy, preoccupied with germs, and often reluctant to associate with other people for fear of catching a disease. In the medieval (but still widely held) belief system of the four humors or temperaments (sanguine, phlegmatic, choleric, and melancholic), the location of melancholy was thought to be under the breastbone and ribs.

**HYPOTHERMIA** is a concern of mountain climbers, hikers, sailors, or anyone who must survive outside in cold or wet weather with insufficient clothing or protection from the elements. Warm-blooded birds and mammals, including man, lose body heat in a cool environment and gain body heat by activities that burn calories. Normal body temperature for humans is 98.6 degrees F. (One degree plus or minus can be normal.) In cold weather, exercise, warm clothing, and food all help to maintain a healthy temperature.

**HYPOCRITICAL** (HIPpo-CRÍTical) refers to people who vocally support popularly accepted values or pretend to maintain standards that they do not hold for themselves in their private lives. This term frequently applies to politicians who profess certain principles when they are campaigning but have no intention of governing in ways consistent with those principles. They are **HYPOCRITES** (HÍPpo-crits). People with records of truthfulness and integrity can defeat them. Well-informed citizens can tell the difference.

A **HYPOTHESIS** (hy-POTH-e-sis) is an unproven position which someone may research to find whether there is evidence to support the position. Many cosmetics are labeled **HYPOALLERGENIC**, meaning they have been created without ingredients which might cause an allergic reaction.

© 2003 J&J Lundquist

# super

**LATIN**

### [SOO pair]    on top, above, over

**super** – situated above or upon; higher in rank or quality

**insuperable** (in L. - not) – incapable of being overcome or surmounted

**supervise** (video L. - see, Vol. I, p. 14) – to oversee

**superfluous** (fluere L. - to flow) – exceeding what is necessary

**supercilious** (cilium L. - eyelid) – coolly and patronizingly haughty

**survive** (vivo L. - live, Vol. I, p. 74) – live over or beyond a threat of death

**supersonic** (sonic L. - sound) – faster than the speed of sound

**superlative** (latus L. - carry) – raised above or surpassing all others

**supercalifragilisticexpialidocious** – indescribably fabulous; from a nonsense word coined by P. L. Travers in *Mary Poppins*

**TEACHING NOTES:** The *Oxford English Dictionary* contains six pages just on the prefix **SUPER** before it begins to cover any other words that start with **SUPER** or those derived from it. It is a very BIG word in the English language. In addition to those listed above, other derivatives of **SUPER** are **SOPRANO, SOVEREIGN, SUPERB, SUPERIORITY, SUPERNAL, SUPREMACY,** and **SUPREME**, just to name a few. The task of listing them all here would be **INSUPERABLE**!

**SUPERCILIOUS** people look down on others from an imagined **SUPERIOR** position, allowing themselves to "raise an eyebrow at" or speak condescendingly to others. **SUPERVISORS** who take a **SUPERCILIOUS** attitude toward their employees will not inspire respect or willing cooperation from those they oversee.

If one pictures a river overflowing its banks or someone continuing to pour water into a glass already filled to the brim, those mental images provide the metaphoric meaning of **SUPERFLUOUS**. Whatever is extra, or over and above that which is necessary, is called **SUPERFLUOUS**. This should not be confused with, or applied to, someone performing a task "above and beyond the call of duty," which means that someone expended great effort, above what is expected, to ensure a better-than-ordinary outcome.

**SUPERSONIC** jets travel at speeds faster than the speed of sound. Seattle's NBA basketball team is called the **SUPERSONICS**. One reason is that, when they were named, the Boeing Company, manufacturer of many supersonic jets, was headquartered in Seattle.

Something is **SUPERLATIVE** when it is the best among other similar items.

© 2003 J&J Lundquist

# sub

**LATIN**

### [SOOB]   under, below, beneath

**subscription** (<u>scribere</u> L. - to write) – sign one's name on a document in approval or agreement with the contents
**subordinate** (<u>ordere</u> L. - to order) – to place below in rank or order
**suburb** (<u>urbs</u> L. - city) – smaller district outside a larger city or town
**submarine** (<u>mare</u> L. - sea) – ship which goes underwater in the ocean
*sub rosa* (<u>rosa</u> L. - rose) – "under the rose" – confidential, secret
**substitute** (<u>statuere</u> L. - set up, erect) – a person or thing acting or serving in place of another
**subterranean** (<u>terra</u> L. - land) – underground
**subduction** (<u>ducere</u> L. - to lead, draw) – collision of two of the earth's crustal plates causing one plate to go under the other

**TEACHING NOTES:** Since the Latin phrase **SUB ROSA** is used so widely to mean "secret or confidential," it's surprising that few people know how it got started. Roses have been cultivated for over 5,000 years. The Romans grew them, loved them, and used them as decoration at banquets. If roses were hung over the table, or used as centerpieces, the guests understood that any conversation heard at the banquet was not to be repeated. It was to be held in strictest confidence. Breaking that confidence meant you would no longer be trusted. Secrecy is just one of many meanings which have been attached to roses.

We think of a **SUBSCRIPTION** primarily as paying to have magazines or newspapers sent to us periodically—daily, weekly, or monthly (and so they are called "periodicals"). However, **SUBSCRIBING** simply means adding your name to a list, whether it be a list of donors to a charity or political campaign, or signers on a document showing approval of the contents. The signers of the Declaration of Independence were its **SUBSCRIBERS**.

There are so many words using the root word **SUB**, it would be a good contest to see who could compile the longest list, along with their meanings, of course.

The term **SUBDUCTION** can open up the whole subject of the movement of landmasses on the earth. The continental plates shift and bump into their neighbors, requiring one of them to duck under at the point of collision and the other to rise up and override the other, creating hills and mountains and sometimes considerable tremor and trauma! The movement along the San Andreas Fault in California caused the great San Francisco earthquake of 1906. Most children will find land movements fascinating. Discussion can open up the whole subject of the natural phenomena of our living earth and perhaps help prepare the children for earthquakes and other such natural phenomena.

© 2003 J&J Lundquist

# rumpo ruptum

LATIN

**[ROOM po, ROOP toom]    break, burst, split**

abrupt (ab L. - from) – broken off without preparation or warning
bankrupt (banca *Italian* - bench) – reduced to financial ruin
corrupt (con L. - with) – change from good to bad morals, manners, or actions
disrupt (dis L. - apart) – break apart; throw into disorder
interrupt (inter L. - between) – break into a conversation or action
erupt (e, ex L. - out of) – break out; burst forth
rupture – break, burst; breach of peace, war; tearing of body tissue

**TEACHING NOTES:** This word **RUMPO, RUPTUM** (especially if you roll the R when you pronounce it) provides a great opportunity to introduce the poetic device of *onomatopoeia*, a favorite of children everywhere. The Greek words *onoma* (name) + *poiein* (to make) were combined to create a word for the process of naming a thing or action by a vocal imitation of the sound associated with it. Some onomatopoetic words are: crash, hiss, buzz, rumble, and **errrrrrruption!** (Old Mt. Vesuvius couldn't have said it any better!)

When you introduce those derivatives on the blackboard, you might ask the students to write a paragraph demonstrating one of them. They are all words for extremely destructive processes and situations, but it is important to understand them. Perhaps it would be useful to discuss, at the same time, the fact that moneylenders used to set up shop at a bench or table in the open marketplace (which explains the "bank" in **BANKRUPTCY**). Explore, too, the ways in which one might avoid **BANKRUPTCY**, or fight **CORRUPTION**. Perhaps the students could identify the kinds of behavior which tend to **DISRUPT** the class. Talk civilly about the need for each person to be able to express his or her ideas without **INTERRUPTION** or unmannerly contradiction. Try to identify people in public or private life whom the students regard as **INCORRUPTIBLE** and why. This would be a good time to tell the traditional story of the Roman, Cincinnatus, who was appointed dictator in 458 B.C. and sent to rescue Minucius, the Consul, from attack in battle. He defeated the enemy, rescued Minucius, and then, refusing to take power for himself, resigned his dictatorship and returned to his farm. A city in Ohio is named for him!

© 2003 J&J Lundquist

# pax pacis

### [PAHKS, PAH kiss]   peace

peace – freedom from war or civil disorder, lack of disturbance
appease (ad L. - to, Vol. I, p. 20) – to bring to peace by negotiating with an aggressor and giving something in return for it
pacifist – one who declines to fight and seeks peace by other means
pacific – characterized by peace or calm
pay – to "make peace" by giving someone what is owed to him
payment – what must be given in exchange for goods or services
taxpayer – citizen who must pay taxes in order to avoid penalties
Pax Romana – the peace which existed between nations which were part of the Roman Empire

**TEACHING NOTES:** The Portugese explorer Magellan, after crossing through a narrow passage at the southern tip of South America (now called the Strait of Magellan), discovered that the ocean on the other side of the continent was much calmer and easier to navigate than the frequently stormy Atlantic Ocean. He therefore named the body of water the **PACIFIC** Ocean. Magellan's trip, an attempt to discover a direct route to the Spice Islands (in the eastern part of Indonesia), was the first positive proof for Europeans that the world was round, not flat. Perhaps a student would like to research his voyage and report to the class.

**PACIFISTS** are those who decline to fight on religious or moral grounds. The Quaker religion was founded by George Fox of England in 1647. The Quaker name began as an insult to Fox who had told a judge to "tremble at the Word of the Lord." His church was called The Religious Society of Friends. In 1682, William Penn founded the colony of Pennsylvania in America as a haven for persecuted English Quakers. Declining to go to war, pacifists are also called conscientious objectors.

Neville Chamberlain, Prime Minister of England, tried to **APPEASE** Adolph Hitler and Nazi Germany in 1938 by accepting Hitler's invasion of the German-speaking areas of Czechoslovakia. He made an agreement which was to achieve "**PEACE** in our time." However, Hitler soon invaded the rest of Czechoslovakia, then Poland, Denmark, Norway, Belgium, Luxembourg, and the Netherlands. Continuing his advance into the weaker nations, France, Greece, and Yugoslavia, Hitler finally invaded Russia, but the Russians resisted him. Britain stood alone against Hitler's Nazi German forces until the United States entered World War II and helped bring **PEACE** to the world. So much for a policy of **APPEASEMENT**.

**EXTRA WORDS:**   **PAX vobiscum**. "*Peace be with you*" – A benediction.

© 2003 J&J Lundquist

# specto spectatum

**LATIN**

**[SPEK to, spek TAH toom]   to look at, see**

inspect – to look carefully at or over; to view or examine formally
spectator – person who looks on or watches; observer
spectacle – public or display on a large scale; an impressive sight
spectacles – eyeglasses
perspective (per L. - through) – picturing depth and spatial relationships on a flat surface; a mental view
perspicacity – keen mental perception and understanding
speculate – to wonder; to buy or sell stocks at the risk of a loss expecting to make a profit
spectrum – an array of items which form a series or sequence, such as light waves forming the colors of a rainbow

**TEACHING NOTES:** The Romans entertained themselves with **SPECTACLES** of all sorts. They built theaters and amphitheaters in all corners of the empire, some of which are still used today for public performances of various types. There is a summer drama festival held in the Roman theater in Orange in southern France. The amphitheater in Arles, and also one in Provence, are still used for bullfights. In Verona, Italy, **SPECTACULAR** opera productions are staged in the amphitheater each summer. **SPECTATORS** at these theaters often bring their own padded seats, since most seating is often on cold marble worn by many centuries of use and exposure to the elements.

In the early stages of the Italian Renaissance, paintings looked rather flat and unrealistic. As artists explored techniques to create more realistic scenes, they experimented with modeling (using light and dark to show volume or depth) and linear **PERSPECTIVE** (where straight lines in the foreground seem to meet at some point in the distance). They wanted to create a feeling of three dimensions on a flat painting. In Leonardo da Vinci's painting of the ***Mona Lisa*** (a.k.a. "La Gioconda") the distant mountains in the background appear to be hazy and less in focus than the lady with the enigmatic smile. This imitates the operation of the eye, which blurs the background when it focuses on something close to it. Leonardo's rendition of ***The Last Supper*** shows his attention to linear **PERSPECTIVE**, as all the lines of the ceiling and the tops of the doors in the room seem to meet in the distance at a point behind the head of Jesus, drawing the viewer's focus to that point and to the most important subject in the painting. Encourage children to experiment with drawing or painting with **PERSPECTIVE**.

© 2003 J&J Lundquist

# VOX
# VOCIS

**[WOHKS, WO kiss]   voice**

voice – sound made by humans through the mouth
vowel – a voiced sound made by air passing through the throat
vocal – uttered, produced, or performed by the voice
vocation – a calling; a career to which one feels summoned
advocate (ad L. - to, toward) – one who speaks toward or pleads the cause of another; a lawyer (slang: a mouthpiece)
evoke (e, ex L. - out) – to call out, summon, bring out; call to mind
unequivocal (un L. - not) (aequus L. - equal) – not ambiguous; certain
vocabulary – the range of words used by a particular person or group

**TEACHING NOTES:** This Latin word **VOX, VOCIS** is the noun form of the similar verb, **VOCO, VOCARE** (to call or summon). They both have to do with the sound that comes out of one's mouth and throat—one's **VOICE**—whether speaking or singing or making other less pleasant sounds! Our word **VOWEL** refers to those letters of the alphabet, A, E, I, O, and U, which are simply sounds coming from a person's throat and open mouth, whereas the consonants represent the work done by tongue, teeth, and lips to change and modify those shapeless **VOWEL** sounds into syllables or words we can recognize.

A team of classmates may like to challenge their friends to recognize a saying or poem when spoken with all consonants **omitted**! Such exercises help children to know and appreciate the component parts of our spoken and written language and to become aware of how much emphasis, cadence, accents, and pauses contribute to our communication. The parts played by facial expressions, gestures, and body language will become clearer as well. Clear **VOWEL** sounds and precisely spoken consonants will make our children more articulate!

Many people refer to the priesthood or to a ministry as a **VOCATION**, something they feel they have been called by God to do, and some artists believe they are called to produce a particular work of art. Cooking aromas can **EVOKE** memories of past family holidays. A good **VOCABULARY** can help **PROVOKE** *discussions* rather than anger.

**EXTRA WORDS:** An **AVOCATION** (ab L. - away from) is something you do outside of a career or vocation, usually for pleasure; a hobby. The Italian phrase *"SOTTO VOCE"* means "under the voice" or spoken quietly, or a private comment not voiced loudly enough for others to hear. **VOCIFEROUS** (ferre L. - to carry) – speaking in a loud voice that carries; noisy or boisterous.

© 2003 J&J Lundquist

LATIN

# loquor locutus

**[LOH kwor, loh KOO toos]   speak**

**loquacious** – talkative; full of excessive talk, wordy
**eloquent** (e, ex L. - out of) – marked by forceful and fluent expression
**colloquial** (cum L. - with, Vol. I, p. 23) – conversational; informal speech
**circumlocution** (circum L. - around) – talking around a subject, evasion in speech
**soliloquy** (solus L. - alone) – the act of talking to oneself; a dramatic monologue that voices inner thoughts
**ventriloquism** (ventr, venter L. - belly) – speaking so that the voice seems to come from somewhere else
**ventriloquist** – one who entertains by using ventriloquism to hold a conversation with a hand-manipulated dummy

**TEACHING NOTES:** Perhaps the best known and most loved **VENTRILOQUIST'S** dummy of all time was Charlie McCarthy of the mid 20th Century. It seems disrespectful to call such an intelligent fellow a "dummy," when he so consistently outwitted his creator, Edgar Bergen. On the other hand, his "colleague" dummy, Mortimer Snerd, a typical "wooden head," coined the slow-witted comment "Duh!" still in wide use today! As entertainers, the trio was a class act!

Hamlet's famous **SOLILOQUY** lets us hear his inner thoughts as he considers what to do. "To be or not to be, that is the question." (Act III, Sc. I.) The **SOLILOQUY** is a theatrical device which Shakespeare used with great effect in the theatre of his day. In modern theatre and film, voice-overs, or pre-recorded "out-of-the-blue" voices, often provide an insight into a character's unspoken thoughts. Watch for them!

Politicians are sometimes **ELOQUENT** (thanks to good speechwriters), and almost always masters of **CIRCUMLOCUTION**, using a great many words to talk around a subject without giving specific answers.

Within any country, different regions may have their own distinctive way of speaking. In the United States you can identify where people come from by listening to their accents, whether they are from the Deep South, Texas, California, or New York. This regional speech may include **COLLOQUIALISMS**, words or terms which only the locals know and use. If you were to say, *"Ah'm fixin' to go to the sto-uh,"* in the North, you might get a strange look, but any Texan would know what you meant!

George Bernard Shaw's play ***Pygmalion*** and the musical based on it, ***My Fair Lady***, create an entertaining situation contrasting the difference between upper class, correct English speech, and the free-wheeling, raucous Cockney **COLLOQUIALISMS** of Eliza Doolittle. These entertainments are *"abso-bloomin'-lutely"* amusing and instructive!

© 2003 J&J Lundquist

# felix felicis

**[FAY leeks, fay LEE kiss]    happy**

felicity – the quality or state of being happy
Felicia – girl's name
Felix – boy's name (and sometimes cats!)
felicitations – happy greetings
felicitous – happily apt or appropriate; pleasantly suitable
felicify (facio L. - make) – to render or make happy

**TEACHING NOTES:** The word **FELIX** is not to be confused with the word **FELES**, meaning cat (see page 2). It would be possible to confuse the two, since **FELIX** has been a popular name for pet cats for centuries (Remember the Disney film *Pinocchio*?) much as **FIDO**, meaning faithful, has been a favorite name for pet dogs. These names seemed appropriate because the loyalty of dogs is so often considered their most important characteristic. Cats, on the other hand, adopt humans who feed and care for them. They ingratiate themselves by purring contentedly and stretching luxuriously on the comfortable laps of their chosen humans. Viewed in profile, the mouths of cats seem to be formed into a perpetually satisfied smile no matter where in the world or in which ethnic culture they have found homes.

We must also remember the great German composer, **FELIX** Mendelssohn, who began composing as a child and at the age of seventeen wrote an orchestral overture *A Midsummer Night's Dream* based on Shakespeare's play of the same name. The "Wedding March," composed for the same play, is one of the best known compositions in history and played at most weddings even today (not "Here comes the bride," the well-known Wagnerian wedding march from *Lohengrin*, but the one played at the conclusion of the wedding as a recessional and appropriate launch into the reception for rejoicing and congratulations). Mendelssohn's *Scottish Symphony* and *Italian Symphony*, as well as his *Violin Concerto in E minor*, are concert favorites all over America and Europe. Why not play some of his happy work for the students? Perhaps a group will want to find out more about his life.

In the 17th, 18th, 19th, and 20th centuries, a baby girl was frequently given a name which described the characteristic her parents most wanted her to express. Along with such names as Patience (the daughter of the Pilgrim father, William Brewster), Constance, and Hope, **FELICITY** and another derived form, **FELICIA**, are very popular even today. All parents want their daughters to be happy, and this name may also express their own happiness at her joining the family. The American Girl series of dolls named the doll from the American Revolutionary period **FELICITY**.

© 2003 J&J Lundquist

# fides

### [FIH days]   faith, trust

fidelity – strict observance of promises; loyalty; accuracy of sound or image recording
Fido – favorite name for dogs, who are known as faithful
bona fide (bonus L. - good) – in good faith; genuine
confide – to trust to the charge or knowledge of another
confidence – belief that someone is trustworthy or reliable
affidavit – written declaration or oath before an authorized official
fiduciary – one entrusted with property or power on behalf of another
fiancé (M) or fiancée (F) (*French*) – someone who has pledged faith to another; engaged to be married
*Semper Fidelis* (semper L. - always) – "Always Faithful"

**TEACHING NOTES:** The universal need and desire for someone or something to trust is as old as the need to survive. Hunting together, gathering food, providing for the birth and growth of children, defending against predators, and simply enjoying the comfort of companionship are necessities of many species of earth's inhabitants. Wolves live in packs, birds in flocks, and cattle in herds. They share sources of food with each other and, except in instances of perceived ill will (or periodically to establish hierarchy), generally do not harm others of their own kind.

Early man began to live in groups even before they settled down and began farming crops and forming communities. **FIDELITY**, or trustworthiness, was a condition for membership in a group then, and it is as vital today as it was thousands of years ago. We all need friends and family in whom we can **CONFIDE**. We need bankers, insurance and investment advisors, and public servants who are honest and responsible **FIDUCIARIES**, and political leaders who deserve our **CONFIDENCE**. We even need dogs who may not be named "**FIDO**" but who deserve to be!

The Latin phrase **SEMPER FIDELIS** is the motto of the United States Marine Corps. It is often shortened to **SEMPER FI** and used as a greeting among fellow marines to show solidarity with each other in the mission of defending the nation. John Philip Sousa wrote a march entitled ***Semper Fidelis***, which is the official musical march of the Marine Corps. Children enjoy listening (and marching) to this and other marches by Sousa.

High **FIDELITY** equipment is that which can reproduce recorded sound or video in a form as faithful to the original as possible. While old record players were often referred to as "the Hi-Fi," modern equipment reproduces sound with much less distortion and noise than the old vinyl and needle dinosaurs. ***Adeste Fideles!***, a popular Christmas carol written by John Francis Wade in 1751, was translated from Latin into English ("O Come, All Ye Faithful!") by Frederick Oakley in 1841.

© 2003 J&J Lundquist

LATIN

# solus

### [SOH loos]   alone, only

solo – an act performed by one person; to pilot an airplane by oneself
soloist – a person who performs a solo
solitary – without companions
sole – being the only one
solitude – state of living alone; seclusion
soliloquy (loquor L. - to speak) – speech in a drama in which a character, alone, discloses his or her innermost thoughts
solitaire – any of various card games for one person

**TEACHING NOTES:** In learning to fly an airplane, the great day finally arrives when a flight student can **SOLO**, or fly the plane alone without an instructor or trainer! (Yes, the word can be used as a verb.) Pilots consider **SOLOING** to be a major event and an exhilarating moment!

A **SOLOIST** is a single singer or instrumentalist, whether he or she be a soprano, alto, tenor, baritone, bass, or a flutist, pianist, violinist, or other instrumental performer. **SOLOISTS** can play a section of a musical composition with a band or orchestra or can perform in concerts, churches, or any special gathering. A **SOLOIST** can be a dancer who dances alone, whether in a world-famous ballet company or a child's student recital. In ages past, before the 20th century, family members were accustomed to play musical instruments or to sing as **SOLOISTS** for family gatherings before there were such things as recordings, radios, or television for home entertainment. Ironically, such **SOLOISTS** contributed a great deal to the enjoyment of family times together and to family cohesiveness.

In the theatre, there are times when an actor's character is alone on stage and can speak his inner thoughts for the audience to hear. The most famous **SOLILOQUY** in the English language is the speech in Shakespeare's play, ***HAMLET*** in which Hamlet, Prince of Denmark, tries to think through what he should do.

*"To be or not to be, that is the question:*
*Whether 'tis nobler in the mind to suffer*
*The slings and arrows of outrageous fortune,*
*Or to take arms against a sea of troubles,*
*And by opposing end them?"* (Act III, Scene I)

A person with a pack of playing cards can learn to play many games of **SOLITAIRE**, which are fun and mentally stimulating. Most computers come equipped with several **SOLITAIRE** games of varying complexity which can be timed, adding to the challenge and the gradual sharpening of hand/eye coordination. Except when played at inappropriate moments, they are *not* a waste of time!

© 2003 J&J Lundquist

GREEK

μονος

# monos

**[MOH noss]    alone, solitary**

monarch (arché - rule) – a solitary or absolute ruler; a king or queen
monk – a member of a community of men who live apart from society and are devoted to religious duties and contemplation
monastery – a place where monks live
monogram (graphein G. - write, draw) – the initials of a person printed on stationery or embroidered on clothing or towels
monologue (legein G. - to speak) – speech performed by one lone actor; a soliloquy
monopoly (polein G. - to sell) – exclusive possession or control of a product or natural resource by one person or company
monotone (tonos G. - tone) – of unvaried vocal or musical tone; tedious sameness; of uniform color

**TEACHING NOTES:** George III was the **MONARCH** in England against whom the American colonists rebelled. The **MONARCH** in England today has very little political power. The real power belongs to Parliament and the prime minister.

One can often figure out which order a **MONK** belongs to by the color of his robes. Franciscan monks wear brown robes. Buddhist monks wear robes of saffron yellow. Capuchin monks (a sub-order of Franciscans) have golden-brown hoods that are the color of the "crema," or very fine foam which forms on a freshly pulled espresso shot. The drink, cappucino, made from espresso and steamed milk and foam, is named for the color of their hoods. **MONASTERY** comes from the Greek *monasterion*, meaning a hermit's cell, which comes from *monazein*, meaning to live alone. A **MONASTERY** houses, in individual cells, many religious men who wish to live alone and spend their days in prayer. Women who choose this form of religious life are called nuns. They live in convents.

Various catalogs show examples of different styles of monograms for stationery or towels. Perhaps students could design their own **MONOGRAMS**. Actors frequently prepare **MONOLOGUES** for auditions. Older students can gain confidence in public speaking by memorizing and performing a **MONOLOGUE** such as Lincoln's Gettysburg Address, or a portion of Martin Luther King, Jr.'s "I Have A Dream" speech, or a poem, or an excerpt from a play. Stress the importance of voice inflection and projection when preparing for the performance. Students should avoid reciting in a **MONOTONE**.

The objective of the game *MONOPOLY*™ is for one player to control as much property as possible.

© 2003 J&J Lundquist

# rideo risum

LATIN

**[REE day o, REE soom]   laugh, make fun of**

ridiculous – laughable
ridicule – speech or action intended to make fun of someone
risible – causing or capable of causing laughter
deride – to laugh at in scorn or contempt; to mock
derision – mockery, pointing at one for others to laugh at

**TEACHING NOTES:** The derivatives of **RIDEO, RISUM**, while they involve laughter, are often anything but good clean fun. They can actually be used as a form of combat in a civilized society by presenting one's political, business, or social adversary in an unfavorable light and making him or her look **RIDICULOUS**. This tactic, of course, assumes a free society with free speech in which citizens can vote and be influenced by publicity about public figures. In a dictatorship, such **RIDICULE** of the leadership can lead to arrest, imprisonment, or even death.

The great Greek dramatist Aristophanes was a master of comedy and made people laugh at political leaders in *The Knight*. He showed the foibles of foolishly self-important people in *The Wasps*, and even **DERIDED** the renowned philosopher Socrates in *The Clouds*. The French playwright Moliere **RIDICULED** doctors in *The Imaginary Invalid*, wealthy people in *The Miser*, and self-righteous religionists in *Tartuffe*.

Richard Brinsley Sheridan wrote satiric comedies in 18th century England. Mrs. Malaprop, the character in his play *The Rivals*, even today, evokes laughter at the misuse of the English language (see page 15). James J. Kilpatrick, watchdog of correct and colorful English, notes in an article in *Smithsonian Magazine* (Jan. 1995) that Mrs. Malaprop still inspires furniture dealers today to sell "French prevential beds" and tables of "naughty pine." These gaffes probably deserve to be held up to **DERISION**, but the satire is gentle so that we need not hesitate to laugh.

The popular late night television program *Saturday Night Live* pokes fun at public officials or anyone in the news who is enough well-known for the audience to "get the joke." The hosts employ imitation of recognizable quirks of style or ways of speaking, exaggerating them to the point of absurdity and making their victims **RIDICULOUS** or **RISIBLE**.

Of course, students should never be allowed to **RIDICULE** others in the classroom. Fear of **DERISION** can kill a learning environment.

© 2003 J&J Lundquist

# laboro laboratum

**[lah BO ro, lah bo RAH toom]   work**

labor – work, toil, exertion of the faculties of body or mind
laboratory – place equipped to conduct scientific experiments or tests or to make chemicals, medicines, etc.
elaborate (e, ex L. - out of) – worked out in great detail
collaborate (cum L. - with, Vol. I, p. 23) – to work together on a project
laborious – full of labor, toilsome, expending much effort
labor of love – task performed for love of the work or of a person
labor union – association of workers in the same line of work
Labour Party – major political party in Great Britain
Labor Day – a U.S. holiday for workers; first Monday in September

**TEACHING NOTES:** The idea of **LABOR** has evolved throughout history. When man spent all his days simply providing for his own survival, whether alone or in company with others, there was little time for leisure. Most lived lives of unending toil. As life evolved and work in a community became more specialized, some people were hunters, some were gatherers, some were cooks, makers of clothing, fishermen, healers, or keepers of wisdom and tribal lore. The question inevitably arose of who was **LABORING** and who was not? Manual labor is easy to observe. Mental effort and responsibility for outcomes is not.

As life evolved over millennia, modern economics developed. The needs of society in this modern economic system were provided by the harmonious functioning of the four divisions of a modern economy: **Land** (including natural resources), **LABOR** (physical and mental, skilled and unskilled), **Capital** (money for purchasing equipment or acquiring access to technology), and **Entrepreneurship** (the one who recognizes a need and develops the idea for an enterprise). Often in the history of the United States these functions were all performed by one person. Homesteading, cattle ranching, cutting and milling lumber, publishing books or newspapers, making bricks, building homes, ships, wagons could all start as one-person operations. Could any of these activities be called **LABOR**? Could all of them?

It is interesting and valuable for students to discuss what **LABOR** is and what it is not. A firm definition is elusive. Reading to the class Robert Frost's beautifully evocative and provocative poem *Two Tramps in Mudtime* (you can find it on the Internet) may give rise to a thoughtful consideration of this ancient concept and of attitudes about labor.

© 2003 J&J Lundquist

GREEK

εργον

# ergon

### [AIR gohn]  work

**energy** (en G. - in) – the capacity for being active or doing work; useable power

**erg** – a specific measured unit of work or energy

**ergometer** (metron G. measure, Vol. I, p. 4) – device for measuring the work performed or energy expended during exercise

**ergonomics** – applied science concerned with designing and arranging things according to the needs of a worker or user

**allergy** (allos G. - other) – exaggerated reaction to substances, situations, or foods that don't affect the average person

**synergy** (syn G. - with, together, Vol. I, p. 8) – working together

**surgery** (chirurgeon G. - working by hand) – physician who performs manual operations on the body

**TEACHING NOTES:** The Indo-European word, *wergon*, meaning work, filtered down to prehistoric German as *werkam*, later German as *werk*, Swedish as *verk*, and old English as *work*. It branched off into Greek as **ERGON** with the same meaning. The derivatives from the Latin word **LABOR** have more to do with the sense of toil and use of manual skill and effort. The derivatives from the Greek **ERGON** have a more technical aspect.

By measuring how much **ENERGY** is expended in accomplishing a task (electricity or fuel used, man-hours worked, etc.), business managers can figure out how many people to hire or how much it will cost to produce a certain product and deliver it to customers. This analysis, in turn, determines the prices we pay for every product we buy. If the price of diesel fuel (a source of **ENERGY**) goes up, the prices of everything that is delivered by trucks increases. It's important for students to grasp how our economic system works.

Many exercise machines include **ERGOMETERS** which measure the amount of energy or the number of calories that an athlete expends during a period of exercise. The applied science **ERGONOMICS**, also called *human engineering*, is concerned with designing and arranging the things people use every day so the tasks they perform can be done efficiently and safely. Office supply stores offer countless items which have been **ERGONOMICALLY** designed: naturally-angled keyboards to reduce wrist strain, and adjustable chairs which provide back support to reduce fatigue. **SYNERGY** refers to two entities working together which produce a better outcome than the individual elements could acting alone. **SURGERY** is that division of medical practice which involves performing operations on the body itself as opposed to administering drugs and medicines.

© 2003 J&J Lundquist

| LATIN |

# durus

**[DOO roos]    hard to the touch, strong, difficult**
endure (en G. - within) – undergo difficulty or hardship
endurance – ability to last through hard times
endurable – capable of being endured; bearable; tolerable
durable – lasting; resistant to wear or decay
duration – length of time something continues or exists
duress – compulsion by threat or force; hardness; harshness
during – throughout the existence or continuation of
durum – kind of wheat with hard grain used in making pasta
obdurate (ob L. - against) – unmoved by persuasion or pity; unyielding

**TEACHING NOTES:** There are several related meanings for the Latin adjective **DURUS** which are echoed in the derivatives in our list. The most concrete meaning, hard to the touch, described hard substances. The ideas of harsh or difficult are metaphoric, meaning that situations or experiences in daily life place one "between a rock and a hard place." To **ENDURE** implies that hardness within enabled the person or thing to withstand wear and tear or assault and still remain intact. The quality of **ENDURANCE** means the ability to withstand pain or hardship. If one's circumstance or situation is **ENDURABLE**, one can bear it without quitting or "caving in." **UNENDURABLE** pain or circumstances will defeat one or cause one to give up.

Throughout history, man has searched for **DURABLE** substances for clothing, housing, tools, and transport. For example, he found leather for shoes; warm wool fabrics for clothes; stone, brick, hardwoods (like oak and teak) for houses and furniture; iron and steel for railroads; and aluminum and other light metals for airplanes. The search for **DURABILITY** is an ongoing quest.

An **OBDURATE** person is one who is hardened against all entreaties or pleas. Perhaps the meaning is best expressed as, "My mind's made up. Don't confuse me with the facts!"

Farmers in North Dakota raise some 85 percent of the **DURUM** wheat used in the United States. The climate, moisture, and soil conditions are perfect for the kind of hard spring wheat which makes the best pasta: spaghetti, macaroni, lasagna, and the rest of America's favorite Italian foods. The history of mankind's evolution from hunters and gatherers to farmers is bound up in the history of the first agricultural crop—wheat. Type *"wheat + durum"* into a search engine and you will reap a bumper crop of information!

© 2003 J&J Lundquist

# bellum

**[BEL loom]   war, combat, fight**

belligerent – warlike; hostile in intention
bellicose – full of fight; combative
bellipotent – powerful in war
Bellona – the Goddess of War, the sister of Mars in Roman myths
antebellum (ante L. - before) – before the war; when capitalized, before the American Civil War
*casus belli* – (Latin phrase) the cause or reason for going to war

**TEACHING NOTES:** An earlier form of the root **BELLUM**, meaning "war," was spelled **DUELLUM** and meant hostilities between two nations. The old form is still used today in our word **DUEL**, meaning a fight between two people. In the very early days of Rome, or, perhaps even earlier, in the days of the Etruscans, people began to worship **BELLONA**, the Goddess of War, who was thought to be the sister of Mars, the God of War. Some people, however, maintained she was his wife, and others claimed that she was his daughter. Unlike most wives and sisters of soldiers, who kept the home fires burning during a war, **BELLIGERENT BELLONA** waded right into the fight. She was a great favorite of Roman soldiers because, judging from the way Rome conquered every other nation in sight, **BELLONA** usually led them to victory. There was a nice little temple erected to honor her near the Campus Martius in Rome, but it had disappeared around 48 B.C. Roman senators used to meet there to welcome victorious generals home to Rome and to receive foreign ambassadors.

*CASUS BELLI* means the reasons given for going to war with another nation. When the rule of law prevails in a nation, one takes a case to court to settle a dispute, but between nations, where there is no court of law to resolve disagreements, diplomats first try to reach a peaceful agreement. However, if they are not successful, and when all else fails, a *CASUS BELLI* is stated, and the nation goes to war. A person or nation who is aggressive, quick to anger, and always ready for an argument or fight is called **BELLICOSE**.

**ANTEBELLUM** is a term used to describe the period in American history before 1860 when the Civil War (sometimes called "The War Between the States") began. It is used to describe the buildings, furniture, costumes, hair styles, and the technology that were typical of the years preceding the Civil War. This war changed an entire way of life for many people in the United States. People who collect antiques find that many **ANTEBELLUM** pieces are very valuable today. Perhaps students can find something made before 1860 in the family attic to show to the class and tell about its history.

© 2003 J&J Lundquist

GREEK

βαρβαρος

# barbaros

**[BAR bah ross]   foreign**

barbarian – person regarded as uncivilized, savage, or primitive
barbarous – uncivilized, savage, cruel, harsh
barbaric – lacking civilizing influences; primitive
barbarism – uncivilized state or condition
barbarity – brutal conduct; act of cruelty; crudeness of style
Barbara – popular name for girls
rhubarb - (Rheum rha barbarum) – Asian plant with medicinal uses

**TEACHING NOTES:** The Greeks referred to foreigners as **BARBAROS**. When we consider that the countries that were neighbors to Greece were not always friendly, the term was not always complimentary. Customs of their neighbors often seemed crude or even cruel to the Greeks as they thought out their innovations in art, science, and philosophy, and sought to build a government of the people which they called "democracy." The autocratic kingdoms surrounding them came to be considered **BARBAROUS** and their customs and ways of living **BARBARIC**, by which they meant less-than-civilized. Consequently, derivatives came to have more negative meanings than simply "foreign."

With these root meanings you may wonder why **BARBARA** has been such a beloved name for girls throughout history. Books of names say its meaning is "stranger, foreigner." The reason is very likely traced to the story of St. **BARBARA**. She was the beautiful daughter of a pagan father, Dioscorus, who imprisoned her in a tower to protect her. Lonely, she began to study the Christian faith. Upon discovering her conversion, her father was enraged, took her to a mountain top, and killed her. On his way down, he was struck by lightning and consumed. Barbara, a martyr, was made a saint and since that time has been thought to protect people from lightning and sudden death. She is the patron saint of artillerymen. Early on, gunpowder often blew up their cannons rather than shooting out cannon balls. Perhaps St. **BARBARA** inspired the technological improvements which make these weapons safer. Someone may wonder about the barber who cuts hair and trims beards. This word comes from the Latin word **BARBA**, meaning beard, and barbers have always been in the business of making men look less **BARBARIC** and more civilized. Even those civilized Greeks who neglected their beards looked wild and **BARBAROUS**!

**RHUBARB**, as known to the Greeks, came from the banks of the foreign river Rha, now called the Volga. It was grown and used as a purgative. Now it is used as a fruit and baked into tarts and pies.

© 2003 J&J Lundquist

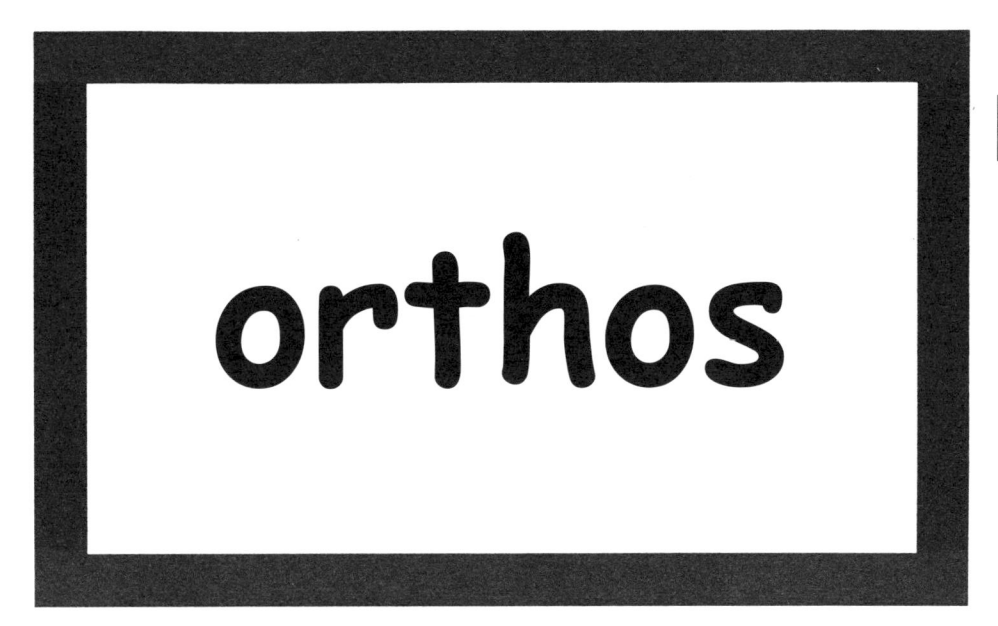

GREEK

ορθος

# orthos

**[OR toss, OR thoss]    straight; correct**

**orthodox** (doceo G. - think) – straight thinking or accepted opinion
**orthography** (graphein G. - to write) – writing proper letters and correct spelling
**orthodontist** (odontos G. - tooth) – one who straightens crooked teeth
**orthopedist** (paidion G. - child) – one who corrects skeletal problems and related muscular problems in children (or adults)
**orthotics** – device for correcting or supporting foot abnormalities

**TEACHING NOTES:** The word **ORTHOTICS** was coined during the 1960s. It describes newly-developed medical devices to correct abnormalities of or injuries to the foot. People who have fallen arches, or bunions, or are pigeon-toed, can have special insoles molded to fit inside their shoes which will correct the problem so they can walk normally and comfortably. **ORTHOTIC** devices are widely used by athletes and others who must be on their feet constantly.

An **ORTHOPEDIST** tries to correct deformities of the skeleton or related muscles and tendons which are too tight to allow for normal growth. They try to correct these abnormalities in children, before they become larger problems in adulthood. Adults also benefit from the services of **ORTHOPEDISTS**, whose expertise is needed to correct many sports-related injuries.

An **ORTHODONTIST** specializes in straightening crooked or irregular teeth for both children and adults, sometimes correcting an overbite, underbite, or spaces between teeth by means of braces. The resulting improvements have helped many people eat more comfortably and smile more confidently.

**ORTHOGRAPHY** involves teaching correct formation of letters in printing and writing, and in correctly spelling the words of whatever language is being taught. If children are taught correctly from the beginning of their schooling, the results are happier and more confident readers, writers, and learners. The time spent establishing these fundamentals is time well spent because, while adults seldom remember their first lessons reading and writing in their native language, they enjoy the benefits for the rest of their lives.

**ORTHODOXY** is the word for the traditional beliefs of a religion or ideology whether it be Christianity, Judaism, Islam, Buddhism, or another. In the face of challenges to these beliefs, **ORTHODOX** or traditional clergy try to maintain the theology or religion in its oldest and purest form.

© 2003 J&J Lundquist

**GREEK**

δοκειν

# dokein

**[DOH kayn] think, have an opinion, suppose**

**doxology** (<u>logos</u> G. - word, study, Vol. I, p. 15) – a hymn containing words praising God

**orthodoxy** (<u>orthos</u> G. - straight, correct) – customary or conventional ideas; approved teaching

**heterodoxy** (<u>heteros</u> G. - other) – not in accordance with accepted opinions

**paradox** (<u>para</u> G. - beside, Vol. I, p. 69) – seemingly contradictory or absurd statement that contains a possible truth

**paradoxical** – contrary to commonly accepted opinion

**dogma** – authoritative system of principles or tenets, as of a church

**dogmatic** – asserting opinions in a dictatorial manner; opinionated

**dogmatism** – dogmatic assertion in matters of opinion

**TEACHING NOTES:** This Greek word **DOKEIN** looks similar to (but predates) the Latin **DOCEO, DOCTUM** which means to explain or to teach. Before one teaches, one must have thought through the ideas or conclusions which are to be taught. A church or a school of philosophy must have formed an opinion about which religious or philosophical principles are closest to the truth, and it must have developed a set of tenets or accepted ideas that are to be taught. Various religions have differing ideas about what is to be preached or taught. The accepted ideas of any one religion constitute the **ORTHODOXY**. Differing beliefs from their perspective would be called **HETERODOXY**.

In the various conjugated forms of the Greek word **DOKEIN**, and in words related to it, the kappa (k) sound changes to xi (ks or x) or to gamma (g). (See the Greek Alphabet page in the front of this book.) So, the use of "x" in the spelling of some of our English derivatives creates these sounds, as you can see in the box above.

The Greek word **DOGMA** is a noun form from **DOKEIN** meaning "that which one thinks is true, an opinion." Sometimes religious teachers have become **DOGMATIC** and have been intolerant of the beliefs of others, forgetting that Truth can be perceived and expressed in different ways. The task of genuine seekers of Truth is to live their lives in accordance with the principles they are professing or teaching and to let the resulting good example do the teaching and the motivating of others to follow their lead. As a current axiom says, "What you *are* speaks so loudly and clearly, I can hardly hear what you are *saying*."

© 2003 J&J Lundquist

# APPENDIX I

## CATS OR DOGS FIRST? YOU DECIDE!

In preparing this book, Jeannie and I delivered several of the pages for "beta testing" to Jeannine Rogel's fifth grade class at Medina Elementary School, Medina, WA. The students had learned many of the words from *Volume I* of *English from the Roots Up*, and were given the task of deciding whether *Volume II* should begin with FELES – cat or CANIS – dog. The students made their choices and wrote persuasive essays, setting out their reasons for their choices. They then held a class debate with an invited audience of students from other classes, teachers, and parents. The fifth graders presented their arguments, and then put the question to a vote of the assembled crowd. We agreed to abide by their decision. We present their arguments gleaned from the five-paragraph essays written by each student, omitting most of the to-be-expected redundancies, but preserving the spirit of persuasive advocacy pressed forward by each enthusiastic partisan. Turn to word #1 to find the winner!

Nota bene: [sic] Latin adverb. so; thus; usually placed within brackets to denote verbatim quotation.

Jeannine Rogel speaks: "On our way to learning Greek and Latin roots utilizing Joegil Lundquist's *Volume I* of *English from the Roots Up*, my class was presented with a challenge that catapulted us into writing a persuasive essay. The challenge was to use an essay format to persuade Mrs. Lundquist to put either *canis* or *feles* as the first word in *Volume II* of *English from the Roots Up*. As classroom teachers know, it is difficult to find a persuasive writing topic that fifth graders have enough passion and information about to sustain their interest in writing a convincing essay. What could be a more compelling issue than one that asks students whether cats or dogs make better pets? The topic was one my students could sink their teeth into without the need for extensive research. This topic allowed students to focus on learning how to write persuasive essays. Not only did the students accept the challenge from Joegil Lundquist, they loved the process of attempting to convince her that their opinion was the deal breaker. It was a compelling and worthwhile exercise, one that the students thoroughly enjoyed. Try it!"

MEGAN A. "Cats VS Dogs - The pressure is rising in Room 601 as the students begin to pour [sic] over their notebooks. ... Dogs are one of the most respected animals ever. But now cats are butting in. Dogs came first! Dogs can serve the community more than cats. Dogs can be expressive in their emotions, while cats just lie around. ... Dogs date back to the cavemen when they were companions to them. ... Without Seeing-eye dogs, blind people would have a much harder time getting around. ... Have you ever heard of a Seeing-eye cat?"

CHRIS A. "Dogs have been man's best friend since 14,000 BC unlike cats. ... Dogs are a lot more fun to play with than cats. ... *Canis* starts with C and *Feline* starts with F. If the book is not alphabetized it would be hard to find things. ... I hope everyone reading this can see that an organized book is a happy [book]. ... Dogs can fetch. They are always energetic and ready to play. They don't sleep all day, like cats. If you can find a cat that can do all of those things, quickly call the Guinness book of world records"

MICHAEL C. "You can be more physical with dogs than cats. For one you can pet a dog and he wouldn't budge but if a cat didn't know you it would paw at you. Also you can wrestle with a dog, though the best part in having dog is playing fetch. Plus how many cats do you see fetching a ball? I hope this convinces you that dogs have earned their place in the world so they deserve it - not cats."

SAMUEL E. "You can go play ball with your dog.... Dogs are great pets to have in a home. Cats might look really cute but dogs are cuter. I think dogs are the best animals because my dog was.... Dogs are smarter than cats. ... My dog sometimes sleeps with me when I go to bed. In conclusion dogs are the best pets in history."

EMILY F. "Cats have been on this earth for a long time, at least since the Egyptian rule. Cats don't require much attention. They take care of themselves and don't need to be taken outside to do their "busi-

ness". ... Cats don't follow you around. They mind their own business. ... If you are a dog lover you might try getting a cat. And if you still think dogs are better than cats you are totally wrong."

CLAIRE G. "I truly think that dogs should be the ones... on the first page in the vocabulary book. ... Dogs are more playful than cats who just lie around and do nothing with the exception of kittens. If you are thinking that you are on the *felis* ... side think to yourself, is your cat loyal to you? Maybe so, but I can tell you how my dog is loyal to me. When I am scared or alone, Pepper my dog will stay at my side and I will feel secure. ... When I want Pepper to obey me she will do exactly what I want her to do, without me... having to show her how to do it. Lastly *canis* comes before *felis* in the dictionary. But if you are thinking that cat comes before dog in the dictionary you are right, but we are talking about *canis* and *felis*. ... When you open a dictionary you always expect and hope that c is before f... and if it's not then you have a really really old or miss printed [sic] dictionary. *Canis* does come before *felis* in the dictionary and you know it, even if you do try and deny me. ... I think dogs should be first in the book and I think you should think that too.

RAQUEL G. "The roots we are debating on are *canis* and *feles/felis*. *Feles/felis* means cat and *canis* means dog. These roots will be in the vocabulary book called "English From The Roots Up" volume two. ... There will be many roots in the book but we are only deciding on the first two. Joegil is depending on us to make this decision, and hopefully we will help her book turn out well. ... Cats have been on this earth since Pharaohs day and age. ... Cats are quiet. Unlike dogs, my cat Cleo can occupy herself if I'm not able to entertain her. Not only that, she is only capable of purring and meowing softly. Dogs on the other hand howl, bark, pant, growl, yelp or do all of them at the same time! ... Cats use the attention they receive wisely. Cleo doesn't crave it and it isn't a necessity for her and she could probably live without it. ... Cats are the most adorable yet walk free animals I have ever laid eyes on. ... Cats are the oldest most respected animals ever to walk this earth. ... So, if there is any sense left in you, vote for cats!"

ALEX G. "Joegil Lundquist the author of an exquisite vocabulary book is at it again. ... The first one she wrote was great and the class learned much from it last year. ... The new one will help even more. *Canis* means dog and *feles* means cat. The majority of the class says that *canis* should go first in the book. The debating will go on in a while and it will be great to know when it is over and who will be first. ... I think dogs should be first in the book. ... Dogs used to be companions to cave men in 1400 BC. They even supposedly originated in America. Though shameful to dogs, cavemen even used them as food too. ... Some dogs even try to entertain you. Like when they jump up and start licking you. ... In conclusion, dogs should be first."

PATRICK H. "I personally think that dogs should go first in the vocabulary. ... Dogs are much more loyal than cats. My dog is loyal because she doesn't run away. She also stands/sits by my side. ... She listens to me. My dog is much more loyal than my sisters fat cat. ... Also she jumps up on my bed and sleeps with me. ... But my favorite quality of my dog is that she is very likable. ... She wakes me up every morning. She also plays fetch with me. ... I think dogs should defiantly go first."

DANNY H. "Have you ever heard the saying 'dog is man's best friend'? Well I think that it is true. ... Dogs help a lot of people in society. There are also police dogs that can smell bombs and illegal drugs. When someone is missing, a search and rescue dog can find people and save their lives. Dogs are amazing animals that can do many things that cats can't. ... Almost all dogs know commands like 'stay' and 'off' to stop them from doing things that you don't like. ... Dogs are always by you so you can teach them. If you tried to teach a cat tricks it would always be gone. I would be amazed to see a cat do tricks. Dogs deserve to be first in the book. ... Have dogs as your top choice."

LEO H. "Dogs are the most loyal creatures on the planet. ...German shepherds. ...are helping the fire fighters...find injured or dead people in New York. ... Suppose, all you cat lovers, if a burglar walked into your house, what would your cat do? ...probably hide in a corner unlike dogs who would die protecting you."

ALEX H. "Dogs, one of the greatest animals on earth. I think that these superb creatures should be first in the vocabulary book. ...Dogs are comforting and loyal. These faithful creatures like to be side by side by their owners and unlike cats, dogs are out going. To me dogs make better pets than cats and are worthy of higher importance. ...If you are sad a dog is what you need, they will comfort you and make you happy. They will do just about anything to make you cheerful. Dogs will go through hard times and good times with you. They will sleep near or on your bed so you know there is someone close that cares about you. Dogs will let you pet them, their fur will feel sleek and comforting as it smoothly glides through your palms. Dogs are the most comforting animals alive. ... They deserve to be first."

MEGAN H. "I think that dogs should be the first page in the Latin and Greek Dictionary. ... Dogs are more playful and easy to groom, whereas cats tend to spend most of their time napping or hiding in a tree or bush. In fact, dogs are thought of as man's best friend. [There] must be a reason why. ... If you put the word *canis* first in the book, the words would be in what seems to be alphabetical order. And it would be easier to find the word you were looking for. ...Plus it would seem a bit more organized. However, if you don't believe it, think of it as a library with books scattered all everywhere. See the difference? Dogs are playful, yet simple to care for. They have the mind and patience to learn more tricks than cats. Dogs come in all different shapes, sizes, and personalities, but completely hairball free too!"

EMMA L. "Dogs are cute, lovable and playful creatures. This domestic animal has been thought of as 'man's best friend' for many years. ... Read on, and I'll tell you why. ... When I said dogs were playful, I meant it. They love to play fetch, and most cats can't even fit a tennis ball in their mouth. ... All dog fans would love just opening the vocabulary book and find their favorite animal. ... It's easy to tell, a lot of people do tend to like dogs more than cats. ... *Canis* comes before *felis* in alphabetical order. Don't believe me, look it up!"

NAOMI M. "Cats are cute small animals. ... Cats are very clean animals unlike dogs. ... Cats are quiet unlike dogs. They don't bark like dogs. They also don't howl at night. ... Cats eat quieter than dogs. ... They bury their waste instead of leaving them there for people to step in. Cats keep themselves clean unlike dogs who need to have people to make them take a bath. ... Cats don't weigh as much as some dogs. Some dogs you can't pick up and cuddle if they are too big and heavy. But you can with cats. ... Cats would be a better pet to carry around. ... Please vote for cats instead of dogs."

MARTIN P. "Dogs are more interactive, *canis* comes first in the alphabet, and dogs don't bring you dead animals. ... Dogs should obviously be first in the book. ... C comes before F. and A comes before E. ... Who wants a vocabulary book in the wrong order? I know I wouldn't want one and I don't know anyone who wants one either. In conclusion, *canis* comes first in the alphabet, and that's the way it is. ... Dogs may catch animals, but at least they bury them instead of leaving them on your doorstep. Cats, on the other hand, leave dead mice and birds on your doorstep. ... I don't know about you, but I hate stepping on dead birds and rats, thanks very much. ... I hope this will convince some cat lovers to change their minds. I hope I don't have to read this in front of the class, but if I do, that's life in Jeannine's class. In conclusion, all I can do is watch, and wait."

MEGAN R. "Cats should be in the book first because they are easier to take care of. You do not have to clean up after them. My cat baths himself. I don't have to feed my cat very much sometimes. Secondly, cats are more beautiful than dogs. They have shiny fur. Their eyes are more radiant. Last but not least they walk more gracefully. ... My cat sleeps with me at night. He snuggles with me all the time. The last thing is he rubs his face against me. All and all cats are nicer.

SARAH R. "Dogs deserve to be on the first page because they are loyal and stick by your side. If someone was trying to rob our house our dog Casey would bark and get them to leave because [he] is very protective [of] our family. ... Whenever I come home the first one to greet me is my dog Casey. ... Whenever I feel like going for a walk and no one wants to come with me my dog will come along with me happily. So you cat lovers, are you beginning to think twice about which animal should come first in the book? My final reason is... that dogs have a large importance to mankind. ... Plus they can find people in burning buildings.

... Another amazing thing they can do is help mankind hunt down robbers with their terrific sense of smell. Now don't you think these animals deserve to go on the front page? If so I ask that you please help me and some of my peers put them there by voting for *canis*.

ANNIE S. "We all hope our animal goes first in the book. We're glad our class gets the privilege of choosing which root word goes in the vocabulary book first. ... Even though dogs are thought of as man's best friend cats have many qualities that should make them be...first. You don't need to tell cats what to do. Cats can take care of themselves. Cats have lived longer than dogs. ... Cats were so valuable back then, in 3000 B.C. that they were thought of [as] gods."

DANNY T. "Dogs are more likable. Gus, my dog, never scratches or bites anyone. ... Telling Gus to do tricks and fetch tennis balls are fun activities to do. ... My dog goes to the bathroom in the bushes. ... That way you never step in it. ... My dog Gus always stays by my side and protects me by fighting other dogs. ... When I'm at school Gus sits at the gate all day with an exception of eating and drinking until I get home. ... It's a very pleasant thing you'd never see a cat do. ... Dogs are up there with the most helpful creatures and cats are just kind of cute. ...Those are some reasons dogs are better than cats so therefore should go first in the book. If you think cats should, hopefully you changed your mind."

CAM W. "First of all some dogs can help people with their everyday challenges. ... Hunters would have to find their game themselves and then get their animal after they kill it if there was no such thing as hunting dogs. ... One of the most fun animals on this planet is a dog. ... If you want to give the dog a workout and you want to throw the ball you can play fetch. ... Also if you want to play with the dog you just have to call their name and they will come to you. Dogs are so much fun! This will be a tight debate with a lot of people for *canis* and some for *feles*. Hopefully I have persuaded you enough that you think *canis* should be first."

SHERVIN Y. "Dogs, one of the greatest creatures on Earth. I think these superb animals should be first. ... First of all, dogs can learn to do tricks. Roll over, fetch, sit, you name it, they will know it. Whenever you go in the park and you are playing baseball with a friend, once the ball goes out they will grab it and return it. ... Second of all these amazing animals are protective. Dogs will start barking at anybody who they have never seen before and well that could help but if it's a friend you could let them know it's a friend. ... Unlike some pets that's [sic] name start with c and ends with ats these animals are a perfect pet no matter what you act like and who you are. ... Dogs should be first."

ERIC Y. "Dogs! Dogs! Dogs! That's what these loyal animals are. ... Dogs will protect you from robbers, crooks, and bullies – cats will never do that, of course. Sophisticated animals, which are called dogs, are very playful. They will greet you at the door every day. ... An animal with such power should defiantly be first in the vocabulary book. I'm for *canis* or dog all the way."

# APPENDIX II

## Alphabetical Index to roots in VOLUME I of
## ENGLISH FROM THE ROOTS UP – including definition and (page number in Vol. I).

### LATIN ROOTS IN VOLUME I

**AD** - to, toward (20)
**AMO** - love (100)
**ANNUS** - year (60)
**AQUA** - water (49)
**ARBOR, ARBORIS** - tree (66)
**ARS, ARTIS** - art, skill (72)
**BONUS** - good (50)
**BRACCHIUM** - arm (30)
**CAPUT, CAPITIS** - head (27)
**CENTUM** - hundred (43)
**CORPUS, CORPORIS** - body (32)
**CUM** - with, together (23)
**CURRO, CURSUM** - run (88)
**DECEM** - ten (42)
**DENS, DENTIS** - tooth (31)
**DICO, DICTUM** - speak (94)
**DIGITUS** - finger (26)
**DISCIPULUS** - student (98)
**DORMIO, DORMITUM** - sleep (58)
**DUO** - two (34)
**FACIO, FACTUM** - make, do (91)
**FIGO, FIXUM** - attach (24)
**FRATER, FRATRIS - brother (80)**
**IGNIS** - fire (46)
**INTER** - between (70)
**JACIO, JACTUM** - throw (21)
**JUNGO, JUNCTUM** - join (25)
**LIBER, LIBRI** - book (96)
**LUNA** - moon (53)
**MAGNUS** - large, big (77)
**MANUS** - hand (28)
**MATER, MATRIS** - mother (79)
**MILLE** - thousand (44)
**NOMEN, NOMENIS** - name (17)
**NOVEM** - nine (41)
**OCTO** - eight (40)
**PATER, PATRIS** - father (78)
**PES, PEDIS** - foot (29)
**PLICO, PLICATUM** - fold (93)
**PONO, POSITUM** - put, place (22)
**POPULUS** - people (82)
**PRAE** - before (19)
**PRO** - before, for (18)
**QUATTUOR** - four (36)
**QUINQUE** - five (37)
**SCIO, SCITUM** - know (97)
**SCRIBO, SCRIPTUM** - write (92)
**SEPTEM** - seven (39)
**SEX** - six (38)
**SOL** - sun (52)
**SONUS** - sound (12)

**STELLA** - star (64)
**TEMPUS, TEMPORIS** - time (68)
**TERRA** - land (57)
**TRANS** - across (55)
**TRES** - three (35)
**UNUS** - one (33)
**URBS, URBIS** - city (84)
**VERBUM** - word (16)
**VERTO, VERSUM** - turn (90)
**VIDEO, VISUM** - see (14)
**VIVO, VICTUM** - live (74)
**VULCANUS** - god of fire (47)

### GREEK ROOTS IN VOLUME I

**ASTRON** - star (63)
**AUTOS** - self (86)
**BIBLOS** - book (95)
**BIOS** - life (73)
**CHRONOS** - time (67)
**DEMOS** - people (81)
**DENDRON** - tree (65)
**DIA** - across, through (54)
**GEO** - earth (56)
**GRAPH** - write, draw (2)
**HELIOS** - sun (51)
**HYDROS** - water (48)
**HYPNOS** - sleep (59)
**KINESES** - movement (10)
**LITHOS** - stone (61)
**LOGOS** - word, study (15)
**MEGAS** - large, big (76)
**METRON** - measure (4)
**MIKROS** - small (75)
**PARA** - beside (69)
**PATHOS** - feeling (85)
**PETROS** - stone, rock (62)
**PHILIA** - love (6)
**PHOBOS** - fear (7)
**PHONE** - sound (11)
**PHOTOS** - light (1)
**POLIS** - city (83)
**PYRO** - fire (45)
**SAUROS** - lizard (99)
**SKOPEO** - see, look (13)
**SYN** - with, together (8)
**TECHNE** - art, skill (71)
**TELE** - far away (3)
**THERMOS** - heat (87)
**THESIS** - put, place (9)
**TROPOS** - turn (5)
**ZOON** - animal (89)

© 2003 J&J Lundquist

# Selected Bibliography

***Webster's New International Dictionary of the English Language, Second Edition. Unabridged.*** Springfield, Massachusetts: G. & C. Merriam Company, Publishers, 1943

***The Oxford English Dictionary, Second Edition.*** (20 Volume Set). Oxford, England: Oxford University Press, 1989

***The Oxford History of the Classical World,*** Oxford, England: Oxford University Press, 1986

Miller, Madeline S., and J. Lane Miller. ***Harper's Bible Dictionary.*** New York: Harper and Brothers Publishers, 1952

Wohlberg, Joseph. ***201 Latin Verbs.*** New York: Barron's Educational Series, 1964

Schaeffer, Rudolf F., Ph.D. ***Latin-English Derivative Dictionary.*** Miami University Press, Oxford, Ohio: American Classical League, 1960

Schaeffer, Rudolf F., Ph.D. ***Greek-English Derivative Dictionary.*** Miami University Press, Oxford, Ohio: American Classical League, 1963

Hammond, N.G.L., and H.H. Scullard, eds. ***The Oxford Classical Dictionary.*** Oxford, England: Oxford University Press, 1970

Thorne, J.O. and T.C. Collocott, eds. ***Chambers Biographical Dictionary.*** Edinburgh, Scotland: W. & R. Chambers Ltd., 1984

Simpson, D.P., M.A. ***Cassell's Latin Dictionary.*** New York: Macmillan Publishing Co., 1962

Liddell, H.G. ***An Intermediate Greek-English Lexicon.*** New York: American Book Company, 1988

Grummel, William C. ***English Word Building from Latin and Greek.*** Palo Alto, California: Pacific Books, Publishers, 1961

***The World Book Encyclopedia.*** Chicago, Illinois: Field Enterprises Educational Corporation, 1975

Halsey, Charles S., A.M. ***An Etymology of Latin and Greek.*** New York: Aristide D. Caratzas, Publisher, 1983

Conway, R.S., F.B.A. ***The Making of Latin.*** New York: Aristide D. Caratzas, Publisher, 1983

Skeat, Rev. Walter W. ***A Concise Etymological Dictionary of the English Language.*** Oxford, England: Oxford University Press, 1882

Shipley, Joseph T. ***Dictionary of Word Origins.*** New York: Philosophical Library, Inc., 1945

# Selected Bibliography - continued

Moore, Bob and Maxine Moore. *Dictionary of Latin and Greek Origins.* New York: by arrangement with NTC/Contemporary Publishing Group, 1997, Barnes and Noble Books, 2000

Scarre, Chris. *Chronicle of the Roman Emperors.* London, England: Thames and Hudson, Ltd., 1995

Landes, D. S. *Revolution in Time: Clocks and the Making of the Modern World.* New York: Barnes and Noble Books, 1983

D'Aulaire, Ingri and Edgar Parin d'Aulaire. *D'Aulaires' Book of Greek Myths.* New York: Doubleday, 1962

*New Larousse Encyclopedia of Mythology.* London, England: The Hamlyn Publishing Group, Ltd., 1959

Etheredge, Samuel Norfleet, selected and ed. *Poetry for a Lifetime.* Orinda, CA: MiraVista Press, 1999

Kent, Allen and Harold Lancour, eds. *Encyclopedia of Library & Information Science, Vol. 7 – Derunov to Egypt, Libraries in.* New York: Marcel Dekker, Inc., 1975

Kent, Allen and Harold Lancour, and Jay E. Daily, eds. *Encyclopedia of Library & Information Science, Vol. 15 – Library Company to Library Review.* New York: Marcel Dekker, Inc., 1975

Holling, Holling Clancy. *Paddle to The Sea.* Boston: Houghton Mifflin Co., 1941

*Nova Online: Shakelton's Voyage of Endurance.* s.vv. "How a Sextant Works," "Navigation by Sextant." http://pbs.org/wgbh/nova/shackleton/navigate/escapeworks.html (accessed July 6, 2003).

*Encyclopedia Mythica.* "Bellona." http://www.pantheon.org/articles/b/bellona.html (accessed August 29th, 2002).

# Teachers – Parents – Grandparents – Librarians
# Students of all grade levels 4 – 12

**GIVE CHILDREN A FIRM FOUNDATION IN ENGLISH VOCABULARY WHICH WILL STAY WITH THEM ALL THEIR LIVES!**

*ENGLISH FROM THE ROOTS UP VOLUME I* introduces **100 GREEK** and **LATIN ROOT WORDS** which you can teach to students from **ELEMENTARY SCHOOL** through **HIGH SCHOOL**, or **ANYONE** who has never had the opportunity to learn them! Just as learning phonics helps children figure out what words are, learning roots helps them understand what words mean.

*ENGLISH FROM THE ROOTS UP VOLUME II* not only gives the next **100 GREEK** and **LATIN ROOTS** with more advanced content; it has fresh ideas, new classroom activities, and new teaching notes. This pair of books will give any student keys to understanding thousands of words in the English language, as well as the confidence to approach and tackle new words he or she has never seen before. You don't need to have a background in Latin or Greek to teach these words. Send for these books today and start teaching tomorrow!

**NOW AVAILABLE!:**
  *ENGLISH FROM THE ROOTS UP - VOL. I*
    or
  *ENGLISH FROM THE ROOTS UP - VOL. II* ............................. $29.95
  Shipping and Handling ................................................. $ 5.00
  Total Cost Either Book ................................................. $34.95*
*Washington State residents please add $2.64 (8.8%) Sales Tax – (Total: $37.59)

Also available,
  Flash Cards (set of 100) for (*EFTRU – VOL. I*) - ..................... $18.00
  Shipping and Handling ................................................. $ 4.00
  Total Cost Flash Cards ................................................. $22.00**
**Washington State residents please add $1.58 (8.8%) Sales Tax – (Total: $23.58)

*Flash Cards for EFTRU – VOL. II coming soon (in 2004)!*

  Please make checks payable to: .................. Literacy Unlimited Publications
  Mail the form below with your check to: .. P.O. Box 278, Medina, WA 98039
  Questions? E-mail us via our website: ...... www.literacyunlimited.com

------------------------------------------------------------

**Please send me the following items:**
                        (please circle Volume Number)
            _____ copies of EFTRU ( **Vol. I** or **Vol. II** )
            _____ Flash Card (Vol. I) sets.

**My check for $** _____ **is enclosed. Please send books and/or flash cards to:**

**Name** _____

**Address** _____

**City** _____ **State** _____ **ZIP** _____

**Phone (in case we have a question about your order)** _____

# LITERACY UNLIMITED PUBLICATIONS
## P.O. BOX 278, MEDINA, WA 98039-0278
### PHONE: (425) 454-5830 • FAX: (425) 450-0141

## Wholesale Price Schedule as of November 15, 2003

*ENGLISH FROM THE ROOTS UP:*
*Help for Reading, Writing, Spelling and S.A.T. Scores– VOLUME I*
    by Joégil Lundquist        ISBN# 0-9643210-3-3

*ENGLISH FROM THE ROOTS UP:*
*Help for Reading, Writing, Spelling and S.A.T. Scores– VOLUME II*
    by Joégil K. Lundquist and Jeanne L. Lundquist    ISBN# 1-885942-31-1

BOOKS:
    *ENGLISH FROM THE ROOTS UP – VOLUME I OR VOLUME II*

| | | |
|---|---|---|
| Retail Price: | Individual Copies | $29.95 |
| | Shipping | $ 5.00 |
| | Total | $34.95 |
| Wholesale Prices*: | 2 – 9 copies | $19.47 ...... (35% discount) |
| | 10 – 24 copies | $17.97 ...... (40% discount) |
| | 25 – 99 copies | $16.47 ...... (45% discount) |
| | 100 or more copies | $14.97 ...... (50% discount) |

(50% discount applies only to orders of 100 or more placed at one time)

*Nota Bene: When a buyer's cumulative orders total 25, the $16.47 price will be extended to all subsequent orders, PROVIDED they are placed for quantities that are multiples of 5. Our books are packed in boxes containing 5, 10, 15, or 20 books. Odd lot orders will revert to the regular price schedule above.*

FLASH CARDS:
    Set of 100 cards to accompany *ENGLISH FROM THE ROOTS UP - VOLUME I***

| | | |
|---|---|---|
| Retail Price: | Individual Sets | $18.00 |
| | Shipping | $ 4.00 |
| | Total | $22.00 |
| Wholesale Prices*: | 2 – 9 sets | $11.70 ...... (35% discount) |
| | 10 – 24 sets | $10.80 ...... (40% discount) |
| | 25 – 99 sets | $ 9.90 ...... (45% discount) |
| | 100 or more sets | $ 9.00 ...... (50% discount) |

**** *Flash Cards to accompany Volume II coming soon, in 2004!*

\* Wholesale prices do not include S&H charges. These will be added to your invoice.

Multiple book or card orders will be shipped via United Parcel Service, so **a street address is necessary**, rather than a P.O. Box.

**We are NOT in a position to accept returns. Please order only what you need.**